DISCOVERING

The River Forth

DISCOVERING
The River Forth

WILLIAM F HENDRIE

JOHN DONALD PUBLISHERS LTD
EDINBURGH

ISBN 0 85976 438 9

British Library Cataloguing in Publication Data.

A catalogue record for this book is available
from the British Library.

Also by William F Hendrie in this series
Discovering West Lothian

PostScript Typesetting & Origination by Brinnoven, Livingston.
Printed & bound in Great Britain by the Cromwell Press, Melksham.

CONTENTS

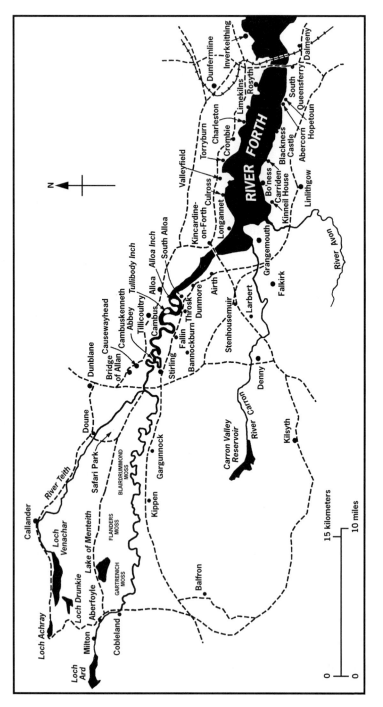

Location Map. Originally drawn by Guthrie Pollock.

INTRODUCTION

The River Forth seems to have flowed right through my life. I was born in a nursing home overlooking the river and brought home to a house in Bo'ness, whose bedroom window enjoyed a view of it. Later the windows of the school I attended provided an even better lookout to watch all that was going on at the town's then busy docks.

It was there that my great grandfather, Matthew McBain, had been the pilot. He died while still a young man through his devotion to his job, when on a gale lashed winter night he insisted on going out repeatedly, in his open pilot cutter, to ensure all the waiting ships were brought safely into the harbour. In the process he caught pneumonia, a severe illness in those days, which in his case proved fatal, leaving my great grandmother with a large family to bring up, single handed. Despite that she found room to look after an extra boy, Bob Miller, who had been left an orphan when his father was drowned in an accident on the river. When he grew up he emigrated to Australia where he founded his own shipping line, whose bulk carriers still ship cargoes of coal to Japan and other Far East destinations.

Perhaps some of my great grandfather's salt water found its way into my veins, because from my time in the youngest classes at Bo'ness Public School I was often more interested in what I could glimpse out of the windows of what was going on at the docks, than what was taking place on the blackboard and still think it a pity teachers in those days never thought of involving us in the real geography lessons provided by the ships sailing in and out of the harbour.

I'll never forget the excitement in the playground one grey morning when a North Sea haar blanketed the town, just as the Norwegian word really means and my classmates and I learned that during the night in the fog, a foreign cargo vessel had misjudged the entrance to the harbour, while coming into port and sliced clean through the long West Pier. At first, as we chanted our tables and did our daily mental arithmetic we could see nothing as we chanced furtive glances through the classroom windows, because of the gloom, but by playtime we could see her stuck fast. After the interval there was even less interest than usual in reading round the class, spelling and even worse, dictation, as we waited eagerly for the lunch time bell and the chance to dash down the School Brae to inspect the damage she had caused to the pier and collect pieces of its shattered timbers as souvenirs.

The weather often caused dramas at the docks and I well remember when high tides swept over the harbour wall and flooded East Pier Street and rowing boats were needed to cross Market Square. High tides also used to breach the single track railway line from Bo'ness to Polmont and I always hoped it would happen on the day of one of my family's Christmas shopping expeditions to Glasgow, so that we would be forced to abandon train at Kinneil Halt and be ferried home instead in one of Davidson or Ainslie's posh black taxis. My memories of the river are also of better summer weather and days when the school holidays were always sunny and burning hot. Then my friends and I again made for the docks to tread warily across the narrow footbridge on top of the big wooden dock gates, with only a single, slender metal chain to stop us plunging into the swirling waters of the sluices below. Health and safety regulations were much more lax at that time. Once across the dock gates we enjoyed our picnics on the shore and told each other stories about the fleet of German submarines beached on the mudflats off Kinneil to await scrapping at P and W McLellan's Bridgeness or Carriden breakers yards. Lemonade bottles emptied and sandwiches all devoured we lingered on the way home to watch the wee paddle tug *Ely* churning up the waters at the harbour mouth or hopefully see the dock diver, with his massive bronze headpiece, disappear into the depths.

My interest in all that was happening on the river was fuelled still further by my father's job at Simpson and Sharp, the well-known Grangemouth firm of stevedores. Our family meal times were often governed by the tides and the arrival and departure of the vessels which his firm was expecting. The earliest paper on which I wrote was the backs of old bills of laden and during the school holidays it was a great treat to be allowed to join him at the docks. My mother was always certain these expeditions would end with me drowned, or at the very least crushed between the buffers of the hundreds of shunting railway wagons, whose noisy clanging and clattering was the song of the docks, in those days.

Lunchtime usually meant a pack of sandwiches eaten on the broad mahogany topped desk in my father's office at Simpson and Sharps, right at the entrance to the docks, just below Station Brae, with its grandstand view of the port, but occasionally there was the added delight of an invitation out for lunch at the famous Galloway's, whose first floor restaurant overlooked Charing Cross. Sometimes after lunch there was time for a quick visit to Grangemouth's fine public library to catch up on the latest shipping news in Lloyds List, always accorded pride of place and spread open ready to be consulted on the big, brown wooden stand in the entrance vestibule. On the way back to the docks my father would always point out the red sandstone Baltic Chambers, in what is now La Porte Place, where my grandfather had his drapers and ships chandlers business and there were always stories of the vessels he had supplied and the skippers with whom he had traded.

I too loved to meet the captains and their crews and an invitation aboard one of their ships was always a highlight of these dock visits. As I poured over the charts on the bridges on these ships, I always dreamed that one of them would sail away with me aboard, but I had to wait until much later to obtain my wish, when in 1967 I at last set sail from Grangemouth aboard the school ship *Dunera* and hopefully infected another generation of pupils with my love for the sea.

In the meantime I had myself progressed to being a pupil at Bo'ness Academy with its galleon under full sail, as its proud badge. At the end of my fifth year having faithfully reported school debates, dances and sports days, I managed to persuade Willie Broom, the owner and editor of *The Bo'ness Journal*, in the days before it was swallowed by the rival, *Linlithgowshire Gazette*, to give me my first holiday job, as an eager cub reporter. Highlight of each week spent collecting the results from the local Bridgeness and Kinneil Bowling Clubs and writing up the coming attractions at the Hippodrome and Star cinemas, was to be allowed to cycle round to the harbour master's office at the entrance to the docks. There Captain McKelvie patiently let me perch on the high stool in front of the leather topped desk to copy from his handwritten log, the names and tonnages of the latest arrivals and departures, the ports from which the ships had voyaged and the cargoes they had brought in their tight packed holds.

DISCOVERING THE RIVER FORTH

Back in the 'Journal's' North Street office writing up the dock news, I envied senior reporter, Winston S Beharrel, who had just returned from actually sailing round Scotland, filing daily reports for the *Daily Record*, on the delivery voyage of the new Forth ferry, *Sir William Wallace*. I had loved the ferries, ever since my mother had taken me to Queensferry as a very small boy and now as a teenager often sailed to and fro on them to Fife. The 'Wallace' brought the little fleet of ferries to four and once I managed to contrive to cross on all of them on the same day, an early indication perhaps of my future enjoyment of cruising world wide. The following summer holiday I was persuaded to swap my cub reporter's pencil and pad for my first experience of life on the teaching staff at school camp, in the Trossachs, at Aberfoyle. There I discovered a very different Forth, almost no wider than a stream, as my young campers enjoyed paddling and playing in its waters below Aberfoyle's little hump backed bridge. Little did I know that I was to return to Aberfoyle every summer since then until 1995.

In the years between, I've written many articles about the river in all its different stages and broadcast on its important and unusual happenings from the whale which became stranded in the entrance lock to the Forth and Clyde Canal to the centenary of the Forth Bridge, which I toasted in champagne as the fireworks exploded over head. I hope therefore you will accept this invitation to come with me as I devote the following chapters to *Discovering the River Forth*.

CHAPTER 1

'ON THE BONNIE SLOPES
OF BEN LOMOND'

Discovering exactly where the River Forth rises high on the eastern slopes of Ben Lomond is difficult. There are so many baby burns, but which one is the infant Forth is difficult to be certain. As they tumble down the hillside the streams merge and eventually form the Duchray Water. Lower down the Duchray meets the Laggan Burn, known also as the Avondhu which is Gaelic for the Black River, which draws its waters from Loch Chon and Loch Ard. It is where these two merge that it is generally accepted that they form the Forth.

As if to confirm this a nearby house bears the name Forth House. It stands at the start of the village of Milton, whose name is a reminder of the days when water power was important to drive the mill wheel and the remains of the old mill can still be seen. From there the river flows east and the land flattens out to form a flood plain overlooked by the grey stone school and attractive old parish church, at the entrance to the village of Aberfoyle.

In the past the flat green fields of the flood plain often did not provide enough space for the waters of the Forth as the river ran high and overflowed its banks, because of the rapid spring time melting of snow on the Ben. Then Main Street, Aberfoyle, itself became a swirling river, to such an extent that the pupils from the school had to be put in boats and rowed home. Today however such excitements are only memories thanks to the drainage scheme implemented during the 1970s.

Aberfoyle grew up because except when it was in spate it was possible to ford the Forth at this point and it became the established crossing for the Highland drovers bringing their cattle south to the annual trysts, the markets at Larbert and Falkirk, where the beasts were sold before continuing their long walk south to England. Today highland cattle are usually brown in colour and indeed are often nicknamed the 'toffee coos', because of a well-known line in confectionary manufactured by McCowans of Larbert. In the past however, they were more often black and as the drovers had to surrender a beast as a toll to each laird whose lands they passed through they complained of 'blackmail', as *meal* was the Gaelic for cow and thus they added a new word to the English language.

No matter the colour of their beasts, driving the cattle through the hills was always thirsty work and so the drovers needed no temptation to stop and quench their thirsts at the inn at the Clachan of Aberfoyle, before fording the river. Years later Sir Walter Scott made the inn famous by choosing it as the scene for the 'affray at Aberfoyle', where the Glasgow Bailie, Nichol Jarvie, saved Scotland's answer to Robin Hood, the legendary Rob Roy from the clutches of the government Red Coats. As the only weapon readily available the redoubtable Bailie picked up and wielded a red hot poker, which was roasting in the fire. To this day a red painted length of metal is chained to the old tree in the garden on the shores of the river opposite the hotel which in Victorian times took on the name of the inn, but sadly this once famous coaching house lost most of its trade during the 1980s. Not even the famous Forte hotel chain who owned and operated it for a short time could revive its fortunes and it has now been converted into houses and flats.

It was from the courtyard and stables, which were latterly the public bar of the 'Bailie Nic', as it was affectionately known, that the horse drawn coaches and charabancs set out in the 19th century to carry visitors into the heart of the Trossachs, when Queen Victoria and her consort Prince Albert through their visits to Balmoral popularised Highland holidays. From the shores of the Forth at Aberfoyle the steep twisting Duke's Pass enabled the coaches to transport these early tourists slowly up into the hills to the Queen's View where Victoria herself had once paused to look out over the Trossch's many lochs, then down to the most famous of them Loch Katrine, which again that master publicist Scott had made famous in his poem *The Lady of the Lake*. On the way they passed the Duke of Montrose's hunting lodge, now the Loch Achray Hotel, which led in the first place to his lordship building the road, which still bears his name.

The name Trossachs means the 'bristly' or 'stoney ground' and although many of the hillside slopes are now forested this mountainous stretch of countryside still lives up to its title. The afforestation has mainly come about since the inauguration in 1953 of the Queen Elizabeth Forest Park, which is named after Queen Elizabeth the Queen Mother and which is now the largest forest in Britain. Its headquarters is the Forest Centre, which looks out over the river at Aberfoyle. Originally known as the David Marshall Lodge, after the chairman of the Forestry Commission at the time of its opening, the centre combines three roles. Its roof top turret acts as a fire watch centre for the area; the main floor provides tourist facilities ranging from an audio visual show about the natural history of life in the forest to display spaces for local craftsmen, while deep beneath the centre is situated a fall out shelter equipped to act as regional seat of government in case of a nuclear attack. This latter use has never been publicly acknowledged even since the fall of the Communists in Russia and the end of the cold war.

Fanning out from the Forest Centre are a number of signposted trails including walks to the Waterfall of the Little Fawn and to the recently restored oak coppice, and one which explains the geology of the Highland Boundary Fault Line. The fault runs through the forest park providing a visually dramatic geography lesson with the rugged scenery to the north contrasting vividly with the softer lowland views to the south.

Looking south from the Forest Centre across the Forth the eye is caught by the white washed Covenanters Hotel, nicknamed the 'Ponderosa' in the 1950s after a cowboy television series of those times, not just because of its unusual architecture for these parts but also because it truly lived up to its ranch style sobriquet as the place where the sport of pony trekking was founded. For almost forty years these treks through the surrounding hills brought many outdoor holiday enthusiasts to Aberfoyle, but now sadly such a leisurely pursuit has disappeared from the area to be replaced by the much more hectic sport of mountain biking. Multi-geared all terrain bicycles may be hired from several outlets in the village including the Forest Centre and the Trossachs Holiday Park to the south on the road out of the village to Glasgow.

While long columns of young pony trekkers no longer wind their way along Main Street, thousands of youngsters do still come to Aberfoyle all year round to stay at Dounans Outdoor Education Centre. Set in a clearing in the Queen Elizabeth Forest Park, the centre takes its somewhat unusual name from the croft which formerly occupied the site. The outdoor centre has an equally

The shallow waters of the Forth at Aberfoyle have always been a popular playground on warm summer days for the thousands of children who have visited the village's Dounans Outdoor Education Centre. This 1960s photograph shows pupils from West Lothian Summer Camp enjoying a swim. Guthrie Pollock.

unusual history. It was founded as an emergency measure at the start of the Second World War, when the government feared that, as in the Spanish Civil War, German bombing raids would devastate cities. In an effort to save the children orders were therefore given to build thirty six camp schools in rural locations including five in Scotland. All were built to the same design with six long wooden dormitory blocks each to accommodate sixty boys or sixty girls, and similar wooden blocks with raked wooden shingle covered roofs for use as dining hall, assembly hall and sick bay. The latest design, in what was described as 'suntrap' classrooms, was attached to each dormitory while toilet and wash facilities were provided in two central buildings at opposite ends of the camp where as described at the time, 'half of the boys and half of the girls are expected to attend the sprays each night'. These nightly shower parades are still recalled by the many Glasgow people who regularly revisit Dounans to recall the wartime years they spent there as evacuees. The first of the little evacuees arrived in 1941 and the camp school was run on boarding school lines

Dounans Outdoor Education Centre has welcomed many young visitors, from war-time evacuees to pupils taking part in environmental studies courses in the 1990s. This picture shows the verandahs added to the dormitory blocks when they were converted to chalets in 1987. The wishing well stands in the foreground. W F Hendrie.

until 1945. While the headmaster and camp manager enjoyed two semi-detached wooden houses well away from the children the teachers lived right beside their pupils in two tiny bedrooms at either end of each dormitory block. 'Build a bonfire, build a bonfire, put the headie on the top, put the teachers round aboot him and we'll burn the bloomin' lot' sang the 'wee vacees' as they were known in Aberfoyle and by coincidence the most dramatic event of the war years at Dounans was the loss of an entire dormitory block not by enemy action but by fire. Although dormitory six was the one nearest the burn which forms the western boundary of the camp and flows down into the Forth, the water from it was insufficient to save the building, only its classroom surviving to stand alone as it does to this day.

When peace was declared in 1945 the Glasgow bairns went home, but Dounans remained in use. At first the Scottish evacuees were replaced by refugee children from the Netherlands. Two years later in 1947 when the Dutch children were also able to return to their homes in Holland, Dounans was handed over by the Scottish Office Education Department to Scottish National Camps which was set up to administer it and the other four Scottish Camp Schools at Meigle in Perthshire, West Linton in Peeblesshire, Gorebridge in Midlothian and Abington in Lanarkshire. Throughout the 1950s and 1960s most Scottish education authorities sent parties of pupils often for whole months at a time. Some youngsters adapted quickly to life at this rural boarding school while others were very home sick.

When they were originally rushed up by the Scottish Special Housing Association at the beginning of the war, the wooden buildings, which make up Dounans, were expected at most to have a ten year life span. Today they still stand, a fine tribute to war time craftsmanship, but although they look much the same from the outside they have been modernised and transformed inside into comfortable, carpeted and curtained twelve bedded chalets each divided into three four-bedded cubicles for children and a teacher or leader's bedroom, both adults and children being provided with full shower and toilet facilities within each unit. Educational ideas and teaching methods have also changed. Most children now attend for short four or five day courses on the environment, ecology and conservation designed to fit in with the Five to Fourteen Curriculum, Scotland's answer to the National Curriculum south of the border. Classrooms are used only as bases for each of the groups and the actual teaching takes place out on the hillside, in the forest or on the adventure assault course or canoe lake, the latter two both constructed by soldiers of the Royal Corp of Engineers during the redevelopment of the site in 1987. At the same time the image of Dounans has changed from school camp to outdoor eduction centre and to mark this the site was officially re-opened by the then Scottish Minister for Education, now Secretary of State for Scotland, the Right Hon Michael Forsyth, who is Member of Parliament for Stirling and who has his home in Aberfoyle.

Some things about taking boys and girls on residential outdoor eduction courses, however, never change and once the daytime excitements of spotting a buzzard wheeling high over Limecraig, or finding a fresh water shrimp in the burn and the evening thrills of visiting the bird watching hides to see and hear the owls and possibly even catching and handling a bat are all over, bedtime stories are still, happily, in demand. Fortunately for the teachers

The Bailie Nicol Garvie on the shores of the Forth at Aberfoyle, with its Gaelic greeting, meaning 'A hundred thousand welcomes'. Once the most famous hotel in the area, and the starting point for many coach trips into the Trossachs, it has now been converted into flats. W F Hendrie.

Aberfoyle supplies its own true tale of the local minister, the Rev Robert Kirk, who believed he could communicate with the fairies. To do so he climbed the slopes of little Fairy Hill, as it is still called to this day. Mr Kirk even wrote a book called *The Secret Commonwealth* about his dealings with the wee folk, but this publicity apparently upset them. As he had predicted would happen, the minister disappeared. Eventually his body was found on Fairy Hill, but this was not the last that was seen of the mysterious minister for he is claimed to have re-appeared at his own funeral. This too Mr Kirk had foretold and had given his brother exact instructions about how he should react and bring him back to life. Sadly in the confusion created by his ghostly appearance, his brother failed to act to save the minister, whose

11

body was subsequently buried in the old kirkyard at the foot of Manse Road, where his tombstone marks the spot.

The graveyard also contains a mortsafe, a grim reminder that on dark moonless winter nights, Aberfoyle was just within reach of the Glasgow resurrectionists. This heavy iron grid was placed over graves in the 18th century to prevent these grave robbers snatching newly buried bodies and rushing back to sell them to the city's professors of anatomy.

Returning to the village over the narrow hump backed little Forth Bridge, perhaps confirms Aberfoyle's Brigadoon credentials but not even that whimsical American musical could conjure up a story line in which sheep become the stars of an award winning live stage show. Yet that is exactly the show biz straw to stardom 'tail', which has come true at Aberfoyle's riverside attraction, the Scottish Wool Experience. Brainchild of local farmer Fergus Wood of Ledart Farm up on the slopes above Loch Ard, the Wool Experience unravels for visitors the secrets of Scotland's woollen industry from the breeding of the sheep and angora goats to the creation of the latest wool fashion garments and the live sheep from historic Soay to modern Merino parade each hour in a cross between auction ring and 'high tech' theatre to enlighten visitors about the finer points from breeding to shearing. The Wool Experience also features displays of wool spinning and weaving, but it is always the animals from the collies which greet visitors at the entrance to the lambs waiting to be fed in the children's farm, which are the favourite attractions for the dozens of coach loads of visitors which crowd the carpark by the Forth each day.

It is somewhat ironic that the buses and hundreds of cars now occupy the site of what was formerly Aberfoyle Station. Imagine the thousands of tourists one train could have brought into the village, but the Aberfoyle railway, was never primarily for passengers. It was built in Victorian times to ship out vast quantities of grey slates from the village quarry high on the Duke's Pass. They were needed to roof Glasgow's blocks of tenement flats and were transported down to the station beside the Forth by a narrow gauge wagon system. The building of the Aberfoyle to Glasgow railway was very difficult because of the flat peaty land it had to cross. To test the safety of the new track the first train to reach Aberfoyle had its trucks laden full of red sand stone on the principle that if it was strong enough to carry this weight, it would be well up to dealing with the loads of slates. Rather than waste money removing the sandstone it was sold off cheaply and evidence of it can be seen in the frontages of several of the buildings along Aberfoyle's Main Street.

Leaving Aberfoyle by the path which follows the route of the old railway track, the line of cottages formerly occupied by the station staff can still be seen, overlooking the well equipped children's play park. The path then follows the line of the Forth as it meanders slowly east towards the Rob Roy Motel. The first motel to be built in Scotland, the Rob Roy soon gained a great deal of publicity, when one of its new chalets was chosen as the place to share out their loot by a gang of Glasgow bank robbers, who were caught in the act.

Opposite the Rob Roy, which has recently been entirely modernised and is now one of the area's most popular tourist hotels, the old mill has been tastefully converted into the luxurious Braeval Restaurant, which is rated as one of the best in Scotland. On the hillside behind it is another of the district's most popular attractions, Aberfoyle Golf Course where visitors are welcome to play its beautiful scenic, if somewhat mountainous, eighteen holes. The course's original little green painted wooden Victorian club house still stands on a knoll near the entrance and pictures on the walls of the bar in its modern hilltop equivalent, show the golfers of the 19th century enjoying their sport.

Back at the Rob Roy follow the disused railway line south and it leads to Cobbleland, the Forestry Commission's attractive riverside caravan and camping site. Further south on the main road to Glasgow the Trossachs Holiday Park offers another excellently equipped base from which caravan and camping enthusiasts can enjoy the area.

The road to Glasgow is carried over the river by a bridge and in its shadow lies hidden the little Trossachs Inn. It is well worth discovering as it is one of the few places where a drink can be enjoyed overlooking the river and with its wide range of malts, is a pleasant spot to rest before continuing on down river, especially on a summer day, when its open air tables add to its delights.

CHAPTER 2
LAND OF THE MOSS LAIRDS

On course from Aberfoyle to Stirling, the Forth historically formed the boundary between Perthshire to the north and Stirlingshire to the south and many still recall with regret the passing of these traditional county names. They were consigned to the waste bin of history in 1975 and replaced by the blandly titled Central Region, an amalgam of assorted parts stretching from Strathyre in the west to Blackness in the east which had little in common and never fitted comfortably together. Now in 1996 the little loved Central Region has in turn been abolished and replaced by the new Scottish Unitary Authorities, of which Stirling is one.

It is interesting to note that over twenty years since the local government reorganisation brought about by the Wheatly Commission in the mid seventies, folk in these parts still stubbornly refer to the Menteith Hills rising on the Perthshire shore of the Forth and the Campsies to the South standing on the Stirlingshire side of the river.

While both sets of hills to north and south add some interest to the views from the riverbank, the scenery along the actual course of this stretch of the Forth is flat and uninspiring as it flows slowly through Gartrenich Moss. First point of interest is the confluence with the little Kelty, the first major tributary to join the Forth and more intriguingly the nearby row of cottages, converted into one spacious house with the name Barbados.

From there the river continues on at the same unhurried pace until six miles downstream it emerges from the peat lands into fertile farm fields. Then between Cardross House and Parks of Garden it flows under the old stone bridge which carries the B8034 to Port of Menteith on the shores of the Lake of Menteith. It is well worth the short detour to sail out from the pier at Port of Menteith to visit the Island of Inchmahome, with its ruined priory where the monks hid the little Mary Queen of Scots until she could be smuggled out of Scotland to the safety of the French royal court.

To return to the river, however, the old stone bridge was built more than two centuries ago in 1774 with money confiscated from

The school built for the children if the Moss Lairds. W F Hendrie.

Jacobite lairds after the failure of the 1745 rebellion. With its three arches, it spans all of two hundred feet or approximately sixty five metres, which somehow sounds less impressive.

Moving on again downstream the river passes a farm called South Flanders, this Dutch name emphasising just how flat and low lying its lands are. On its north shore the Forth then forms the boundary of another farm called Faraway. This place name seems equally appropriate, as to reach it, it is necessary to drive past two other farms and over a narrow box girder bridge. Faraway Farm House was built in such an isolated spot, because it originally possessed only twelve acres of land and it was not until the moss was cleared from the surrounding area that it was able to expand to its present two hundred acres.

It was the famous Scottish law lord, Lord Kames, who was mainly responsible for clearing the area of its mossy unproductive shroud. In 1766 he became owner of Blairdrummond, now well-known as the site of Scotland's only safari wildlife park. Although his new estate was large, covering two thousand acres, one thousand eight hundred of them were covered in a thick layer of springy peat moss, twelve feet (four metres) thick in many parts, which made any kind of agricultural use entirely impossible.

Lord Kames had however, some experience of land reclamation

on his other estates and was determined to rid Blairdrummond of its blanket of moss, because below it he was certain lay excellent rich alluvial soil, first rate for farming. The problem was how to tackle the task as several previous attempts to remove the moss by digging it up had been defeated by the sheer enormity of the task.

Some swifter method had to be found and Kames finally decided the only feasible way was to employ water power to wash all the peat into the Forth. Labourers were hired to dig canals to float the moss to the river, but although his lordship was able to show his idea worked it seemed he would have to abandon the project because of the enormous cost. Just as it seemed Blairdrummond Moss would remain unproductive he came up with a way to get the work done free. For in the Highlands the terrible clearances had started forcing hundreds of crofters to leave their homes to make way for the sheep, which were more profitable and much less labour intensive. Kames reckoned therefore that rather than emigrate to the United States or Canada, many of them would rather find new land to farm in Scotland and that as they were used to labouring outdoors in all weather he reasoned they would be the ideal people to remove his estate's mossy blanket.

Therefore he decided to offer the Highlanders ten acre crofts with guaranteed tenure and freedom from rent for the first seven years, provided they promised to clear their holdings of moss. To tempt the shrewd crofters still further he promised until they could grow food on their land, he would provide them with enough oatmeal to make porridge for their whole families and reminded them they would always have plenty of peat to keep their fires burning.

In 1769 the first of the crofters arrived at Blairdrummond, much to the terror of the local inhabitants, who were as scared of the Moss Lairds as they sarcastically dubbed the Highlanders, as they might have been two centuries later of the modern lions, which now roam the estate. Dreadful rumours spread that the crofters were savages who were frequently violent, especially when drunk, which they were most of the time. To make matters worse the Moss Lairds spoke little English and formed their own little Gaelic speaking community, living in dwellings unlike anything the local people had ever seen previously. These homes were even more

The grounds of Lord Kames's home, Blair Drummond House, are now the site of Scotland's only safari and leisure park. Established over 25 years ago, it continues to be one of the country's top visitor attractions, providing a very full day out for all the family. As well as the giraffe in this picture its animals include lions, Siberian tigers, bears, zebras, chimpanzees, monkeys and two African elephants. The safari park is open every day from April to September each year. The impressive mansion seen in the picture was completed in 1869 and replaced the original Blair Drummond House, lived in by Lord Kames, which was demolished the following year. Throughout this century it was the home of the Muir family, who still own the surrounding lands and the safari park. The house was sold in 1977 to the Camphill Trust, who use it to care for the handicapped. Jarrold Publishing, Norwich.

simple and primitive than anything the crofters had been used to in the Highlands, but for good reason. For they very soon discovered that as a little as a footstep on the moss was sufficient to make it vibrate for up to fifty metres and a stone or brick built house would have collapsed as if hit by an earthquake. It was true Highland guile therefore which led the Moss lairds to cut their first homes right out of the peat moss itself.

How they achieved this is described by Victorian geologist and

Bo'ness coalmine owner Henry M Cadell in his book, *The Story of the Forth*. To start, the Moss Laird and his family dug a deep wide trench right down through the peat right round the site they had chosen for their house. Within the square trench this left a solid block of peat and it was from this that they scooped out their home, just as 'a child hollows out the heart of a turnip to make a lantern', as Cadell graphically describes it.

To begin with the walls of the peat houses were as high as four metres, but as the moss dried out they shrunk until they were only about five feet high and with walls about a metre thick. They were roofed with wood supplied free by Lord Kames and once thatched with the heather, which grew all around, it was difficult to tell them apart from the surrounding countryside. It was hardly surprising the townsfolk of neighbouring Doune and Thornhill were convinced the Moss Lairds' homes were only fit for animals, but the crofters did not worry, because inside their small dark low ceilinged one roomed homes were snug and warm and being so low, were protected from the strongest wind which blew across the mosslands.

Slowly, however, as they won their battle with the moss at Blairdrummond, the Highlanders replaced their original houses with the more usual stone built cottages. By this time too their hard work and law abiding behaviour convinced their lowland neighbours that they did not really have to lock up their valuables and their daughters, as they had at first worriedly predicted. The barriers between the Highlanders and the local people were gradually demolished and the social stigma of being a Moss Laird disappeared, until nowadays it is thought an honour to be descended from such hard working stock.

Lord Kames, who was over seventy when he began his ambitious clearance work at Blairdrummond, died in 1782, but his son George Hume continued the scheme. To encourage the Moss Lairds he built roads to open up the district and provide a link with Stirling. He also provided prizes of ploughs and bags of seed for those who cleared most land in the shortest time. Most importantly he made the Moss Lairds' job easier by building a huge water wheel near where the River Teith joins the Forth, thus making available to them far greater water power to wash away the moss.

Several other landowners around Blairdrummond were

encouraged to copy his example and by 1811 around 150 Moss Lairds and their families, totalling around 950 people, were engaged in clearing ever increasing areas of Bairdrummond Moss, Cardross Moss, Kincardine-in-Menteith Moss and Flanders Moss, the latter of which is now a nature reserve.

The Moss Lairds added to their income by cutting the peat and selling it as fuel in Stirling and other towns in the district. As they became better off they decided that their children must be educated and encouraged by George Hume who paid part of the dominie's salary, a school was opened. Thus over the years the Moss Lairds were integrated into local society. By working hard they were able to afford to buy livestock and lay the foundations for the prosperous farms through whose lands the Forth now flows, as it draws ever closer to Stirling.

Before then the river is joined by two other tributaries, the little Goodie Water, two miles above Gargunnock and two miles above Stirling by the larger Allan on whose banks stand Bridge of Allan and Dunblane.

From where the Duchray and Avondhu first form the Forth above Aberfoyle to Stirling is a direct distance of $18^{1}/_{2}$ miles, but because of its windings it takes the river 39 miles to reach this point on its journey to the sea.

CHAPTER 3

THE LINKS OF THE FORTH

As it approaches Stirling the Forth can perhaps best be described as a ball of blue wool, which has become the play thing of a mischievous kitten. First it twists in one direction, then another and at times seems as if it is actually going to meet itself as it winds backwards and forwards.

These are in fact the famous links or windings of the Forth, which more than double the distance the river takes to flow from Stirling to Alloa from about $5^1/_2$ to $12^1/_2$ miles. For while the links are overlooked in dramatic fashion by high rocky crags on which Stirling Castle and the Wallace Monument are impressively set, the lands through which the river itself flows are so flat that it almost loses momentum.

This is an area of great interest for geologists who describe the Forth's leisurely loops as meanders. This landscape was formed during the last great ice age when the massive sheet of ice moving slowly from the north-west to the south-east, was able to scrape away the soft layers of sandstone and other sedimentary rock from what is now the broad river valley, but was thwarted when it came up against the hard igneous basalt of the Abbey Craig and the Castle Rock. Thus were formed the crag and tail formations which dominate the Stirling skyline. For once the ice was forced to split to get around these solid plugs of black basalt, it took some distance for it to come together again and the narrow strips of land behind the crags became their tails.

Stirling's crag and tail formations to north and south of the Forth look like two crouched heraldic lions guarding its progress to the sea. It is well worth leaving the shores of the river to climb both to get almost aerial views of its course.

It takes 246 steps to reach the top of the Wallace Monument, but on each floor on the climb up there are interesting displays to provide good excuses to pause for a while to become absorbed in the atmosphere of the recreation of Wallace's battle tent and admire the replica of his great double bladed sword. Much of this magic was also caught in the Mel Gibson film *Braveheart*, which received its British premiere in September 1995 at the MacRobert Theatre in the heart of the beautifully wooded campus of the University of Stirling whose extensive grounds occupy the lower slopes of the Abbey Craig. Looking out from the vantage point at the top of the Wallace Monument it is also possible to look down on Causewayhead, far below, and see how this Stirling suburb which was once a village in its own right lies first on the north side of the Forth, then on its east shore and then on its west bank.

High on the Abbey Craig overlooking the Forth is a most appropriate setting for the Wallace Monument because it overlooks the scene of the Scottish hero's greatest triumph, the Battle of Stirling Bridge. Fought in 1297 against the might of King Edward 1st's English army, this was a vital fight for Wallace knew well that whoever controlled Stirling controlled Scotland. The reason for this was that Stirling was then the only place the Forth could be crossed by bridge. To the west, as already described lay the uncrossable mosslands, while to the east the river became so broad that an army would have needed a fleet of boats, which medieval military commanders did not possess.

The old bridge over which Wallace's troops fought the English under the Earls of Cressingham and Surrey, has long disappeared, but even the present old four arched Stirling Bridge has its war history as General Blakeney, Governor of Stirling Castle, severed one of the spans in 1745 to try to prevent the Jacobites entering the town. It was hurriedly rebuilt the following year to allow the Duke of Cumberland to pursue them north again. Just metres down stream from the old, the newer Stirling Bridge spans the river. This five arched structure was designed by the well-known Scottish engineer Robert Stevenson, who was related to the even more famous author and was opened in 1832 at a cost of £17,000.

Just as the Forth seems truly intent on entering Stirling, it winds on again to one of the most tranquil backwaters in the area, the village of Cambuskenneth. So well is it hidden in a grassy green loop surrounded by the river that most visitors miss Cambuskenneth. It is however well worth searching out the road which leads to it from beneath the Abbey Craig, because it is the peaceful site of the ruined abbey where King James III lies buried.

Cambuskenneth takes its name from another monarch, Kenneth MacAlpine, King of Dalriada, but it was the later Sottish king, David 1st, who founded the abbey for the monks of the Augustinian

The fine stonework of the Old Stirling Bridge is seen to full advantage in this picture, which also shows the Wallace Monument. Loch Lomond, Stirling and Trossachs Tourist Board.

order. Today only the abbey's bell tower, which was restored by order of Queen Victoria in 1865 remains standing, but from the foundations of the other ecclesiastic and domestic buildings it is possible to visualise the quiet religious life led by the brothers in this peaceful riverside setting.

Typical of medieval church architecture, their church faced east, so that they and their congregation might pray facing towards the Holy Land and also for the more practical reason that the light of dawn filtering through the tall window in the apse might supplement the glow of candles on the high alter at the first service of the morning. Following that early morning worship the monks made their way in procession from the church to the neighbouring chapter house, whose ruins, like those of the other foundations, have all been clearly labelled by Historic Scotland to whose care they have been entrusted. The chapter house took its name from the fact that at this dawn meeting the monks read either a chapter of the Bible or of the writings of their founder St Augustine, detailing the rules and discipline which he expected his followers to accept and obey. After any misdemeanours had been corrected either through prayer or penance in the form of corporal chastisement, the abbot issued each monk with his work for the coming day. This was divided into three parts for prayer, manual labour and time for reading in the abbey's library or writing in its scriptorium.

Next to the chapter house at Cambuskenneth, as in the priory mentioned earlier on Inchmahome, lay the parlour, a small room whose name was derived from the French verb *parler*, meaning to talk, as this was the only place where the monks were allowed to chat for a short time before meals. Before meals too they would wash their hands in a basin filled with water drawn from the river, as the monks were the first to appreciate the need for hygiene. In this connection also the Forth provided water to flush the abbey's rere-dorter and the site of this primitive lavatory can still be found.

The grounds of the abbey also contain many interesting grave stones, most famous of which is that of King James III and his queen, Margaret. Their remains were discovered in the middle of the 19th century, protected only by a slab of blue marble. When Queen Victoria was informed, she gave instructions for the provision of the memorial stone, which now guards their tomb and whose inscription tells the story of the King's defeat in battle and his subsequent death. The right of James to the throne of Scotland was challenged by his rebellious nobles. Battle was joined at Sauchieburn on 11 June, 1488. Recognising the overwhelming power of the nobles James is said to have left the field before the fighting actually began, but riding his distinctive grey charger was spotted and slain before he could find a safe refuge.

Today Cambuskenneth seems nearly deserted, the few visitors who come being mainly Scandinavian tourists drawn to it through interest in the wife of the Scottish king, who was Princess Margaret of Denmark.

Cambuskenneth was not always so quiet, however, because until 1935 it was at this point that a public ferry plied to and fro across the narrow width of the Forth. The little wooden rowing boat, which made the crossing, has long disappeared, but the ferryman's cottage still overlooks the river. Its last occupant connected with the crossing was Thomas Dow, who took over the job from his father in 1921 and worked the passage for the next fourteen years. Although the crossing was short his days must have been long because the rules for the ferry stated, 'The attendant will be on duty to ferry over passengers between 5 am and 11.30 pm, when required by them so to do. The attendant on duty shall take personal charge of the ferry and shall see that no-one is allowed to row, who is not competent to do so'.

It is intriguing to wonder if the latter clause was included to prevent any late night revellers from commandeering the boat. Very late crossings were not too common as after the 10.30 pm curfew, ferryman Dow was entitled to an additional payment of a silver sixpence (2^1/$_2$p) which was a not inconsiderable extra charge in the 1930s. The ferry was capable of carrying twenty passengers, but although it was seldom that busy in the mid thirties Stirling Burgh Council decided that a footbridge should be built to make it easier for the residents of Cambuskenneth to reach the town. On 23rd October 1935 the Provost of Stirling and the magistrates in their red gowns trimmed with white ermine fur and the other councillors paraded from the south shore to the middle of the new bridge where they met Mr Dow and his wife and the villagers. There as the river flowed below them they conducted a simple ceremony to officially open the new bridge and at the same time close this ancient ferry crossing of the Forth.

From Cambuskenneth with its neat little streets of well tended cottages, colourful well kept gardens and its welcoming Abbey Inn, which provides a pleasant spot to meet the locals and enjoy a drink and a bite to eat, the river meanders on. It seems to forget however that it is expected to flow to the sea, because it turns its back on its eastern progress and decides instead to flow westward, back at last into the heart of Stirling.

The area of the old port is today sadly neglected, but there are plans to build a new route into the burgh from the east, which would follow the old shore road and hopefully bring new life to this riverside site. For the present however, it is hard even with the most vivid imagination to picture Stirling as the bustling busy port, which it once was, but records from the 11th to the early 19th century provide evidence for the trade which it once enjoyed. For all these hundreds of years small sailing ships voyaged all this way up river bringing goods from all parts of Europe for the merchants of the burgh and especially for use at the court at Stirling Castle. Today the brilliantly restored castle kitchens show the full range of foods, wines and spices available to the royal chefs to prepare the feasts served in the great banqueting hall, which is also being restored to its former glory. Sturgeon from Russia, nutmeg from the East Indies and rich red wine from Bordeaux all were shipped up the Forth to Stirling and at one particular feast this link with the sea was specially commemorated when a miniature galleon under full sail was created to carry the dishes and the silver salvers laden with tempting food right into the banqueting hall, much to the delight of the diners.

As well as cargo the ships which plied to and fro all the way up river to Stirling also carried passengers. River travel became a much more attractive alternative to travel overland by bumpy stage coach, when in 1813, as a result of a great deal of interest created by Henry Bell's pioneering *Comet* coming to the Forth for her first annual overhaul, the first steamship service was introduced from the inland port all the way to Granton for passengers wishing to visit Edinburgh.

Appropriately the first steamer was named the *Stirling*. Built on the Clyde at Greenock it was purchased by another Mr Bell, who was no relation of the inventor. With the encouragement of several local businessmen he sailed his new vessel through the Forth and Clyde Canal and successfully navigated her up river to Stirling, from where she began a daily service. She proved so successful that in 1815 he ordered the first two steamers to be built on the Forth. They were constructed at Kincardine and both were launched on the same day. One was named *Lady of the Lake* and the other, *Morning Star*. Soon they joined the original *Stirling* on the service to and from Edinburgh, but Mr Bell had been over ambitious. There were not enough passengers for all three steamers and very reluctantly he was forced to sell his new *Lady of the Lake* to German owners. Three years later however he was convinced there were now sufficient passengers to make three boats pay and so he proudly repurchased his 'Lady', which sailed safely all the way back from Hamburg.

From then until 1826 Mr Bell's fleet flourished, but that year he heard several rival Stirling businessmen were putting up £4,500 to found the new Stirling, Alloa and Kincardine Steamboat Company. As a shrewd businessman himself, Mr Bell realised there were not enough passengers wishing to travel on the Forth to sustain a new fleet of steamers. He therefore approached his Stirling rivals and offered to save them the time and trouble of building new steamers for themselves by selling them his three vessels for exactly £4,500! And so the *Stirling*, the *Lady of the Lake* and the *Morning Star*

25

changed owners and the monopoly of steamer traffic on the Forth continued for almost another ten years.

In 1835, however, the Stirling, Alloa and Kincardine Steamship Company was challenged by a Mr Barclay from Glasgow, who brought the *Benalmond* from the River Clyde. This time neither side would give way and a whole series of riverboat battles soon developed with the steamers of the two rival companies racing to be first at each pier.

One of the battles for custom is described in fascinating detail by an early American travel writer, Mr N P Willis who inadvertently got caught up in the river boat fray, more reminiscent of the mighty Mississippi than the slow flowing Forth. He wrote:

> At Stirling, I had a running fight for my portmanteau and carpet bag, from the hotel to the pier, and was at last embarked in the entirely wrong boat, by sheer force of pulling and lying. The two steamers, the *Victoria* and the *Benalmond*, got under way together; the former, in which I was a compulsory passenger, having a flageolet and a bass drum by way of a band, and the other a dozen lusty performers and most of the company.
>
> The river was narrow and the tide down and although the other seemed the better boat, we had the bolder pilot and were lighter laden and twice as desperate.
>
> Whenever we were quite abreast and the paddle wheels touched with the narrowness of the river, we marched our flageolet and bass drum close to the enemy and gave them a blast, 'to waken the dead', taking occasion, during moments of defeat, to recover and ply the principal musician with beer and encouragement.
>
> The two pilots stood broad on their legs, every muscle on the alert and although the *Benalmond* wore the cleaner jacket, *Victoria* had the 'varminter' look. He was the wickedest of all wicked things, a wicked Scotsman…a sort of saint turned sinner.
>
> As we approached a sharp bend in the course of the stream, I perceived by the countenance of our pilot, that it was to be the critical moment.
>
> The *Benalmond* was a little ahead, but we had the advantage of the inside of the course and very soon with commencement of the curve we gained sensibly on the enemy and I saw that we would cut her off by a half-boat's length.
>
> The flageolet made all split again with *The Campbells are Comin'*. The bass drum was never so belaboured and, 'Up with your helm,' cried every voice as we came at the rate of twelve miles in the hour, sharp on to the angle of mud and bulrushes and to our utter surprise

The links of the Forth, viewed from the top of the Wallace Momument. Loch Lomond, Stirling and Trossachs Tourist Board.

the pilot jammed down her tiller and ran the battered nose of the *Victoria* plumb in upon the enemy's forward quarter.

The next moment we were going it like mad down the middle of the river and far astern stuck the *Benalmond* in the mud, her paddles driving her deeper at every stroke, her music hushed and the crowd on her deck standing speechless with amazement. The flageolet and bass drum marched aft and played louder than ever and we were soon in the open Firth and without competition to the sleeping isle of Inchkeith.

CHAPTER 4
FROM STIRLING TO ALLOA

From Stirling to Alloa by road is a mere six miles, but following the twists and turns of the Forth it is all of twelve and a half. Leaving Stirling, the river flows by the flat grassy area occupied by ABRO, the Army Base Repair Organisation, the army's only repair agency in Scotland. It also looks after repairs for the Royal Airforce and the Royal Navy meaning that it provides a service to 450 units from the Shetland Islands in the north to one in Berwick in Tweed, just over the border in England to the south. In equipment terms it is responsible through its workshops and contract repair organisation for well over 4,000 vehicles, 10,000 weapons, 5,000 radios and 10,000 instruments ranging from heat seeking cameras to remote control bomb disposal equipment. It is also responsible for the world wide overhaul of army Landrover gearboxes and axles and for the servicing of all Bedford 4 ton vehicles. ABRO, which has been entirely civilian operated for several years, also has its own indoor weapons firing range. High security is maintained at all times and so it is not possible to walk along this stretch of the south shore of the river. The sounds of dogs barking is often heard from the ABRO site, but contrary to popular belief the dogs are not part of its security system. The dogs belong to Central Region Police, who have their kennels on part of the site near the bank of the river.

Immediately past the large area occupied by ABRO the river passes one of Stirling's business development parks, one of whose liveliest occupants is the local commercial radio station, Central FM. As its title indicates it broadcasts on the FM waveband and its programmes can be heard twenty four hours a day throughout the whole of the Forth Valley, its pop music output interspersed with local news, weather and road information while its talk programmes range from sport to religion with well-known Clackmannan minister and former BBC producer the Rev Douglas Aitken as its radio padre. Much of Central FM's advertising revenue comes from the new businesses such as the large and impressive new supermarket and the excellent new Forthbank sports stadium, which have sprung up since the mid 1990s on the flat carse of the Forth. These modern developments along the shores of the Forth to the east of Stirling at Springkerse have been furthered by a vastly improved roads network linking this area with the M9 motorway to the south and the main road to Fife to the north. The latter route is reached over the newest bridge across the Forth. Built of concrete, its long low span is architecturally unexciting, but it is a great practical help to local transport. The road bridge, built by Central Regional Council, was officially opened on 14th April 1985 by Chairman of the Roads and Transport Committee, Councillor T G Simpson, JP.

Ten years after its opening the bridge still marks the eastward expansion of new enterprises and on its far side on the south shore the river regains its rural look. On the south shore a farm track leads into rich agricultural land where sheep and cows graze peacefully. The farms include Upper Taylorton and Balfornought.

In marked contrast across the river is the site of the once prosperous Manor Powis Pit. It was supplemented in 1956 and finally replaced in 1967 by the Manor Powis Mine, which was entered slightly further downstream and which at its peak employed over five hundred miners. Its workings ran over three miles all the way to Alloa, before it closed as part of the general decline of Scotland's coal mining industry. How much pleasanter it is to walk the riverbank than contemplate the claustrophobic existence of past miners labouring in the dark depths below.

Back on the south shore the way is barred by the waters of the Bannockburn flowing into the river. This is, of course the burn after which the battlefield where King Robert the Bruce inflicted his world famous victory on the English in 1314, took its name. A detour to visit the National Trust for Scotland's excellent interpretive centre at the battlefield is well worth while.

The waters of the Bannockburn may well have run red with blood of both English and Scottish soldiers on the day of the battle, but it is a much healthier red which leads us on down river. For this according to local tradition is where on the banks of the Forth the McIntosh Red Apple had its origin in the walled garden of Lower Polmaise Estate. Here it is claimed Dr McIntosh cultivated apple trees before he emigrated to Canada. When he sailed across the Atlantic he is said to have taken his apple seed with him and ultimately gave his adopted country one of its most famous

The Bruce, the famous equestrian statue of the Scottish hero, which looks out over the site of the battlefield at Bannockburn, where the National Trust for Scotland's Visitor Centre provides an excellent place for visitors to find out information about the battle.

exports, the McIntosh Red.

The mansion house of Polmaise was abandoned after the First World War, when the Murray family moved their family seat to Polmaise near Bannockburn. By the start of the Second World War the house had become roofless and during the hostilities it was deliberately destroyed during a military exercise. It is perhaps a pity the Royal Corp of Engineers did not turn their talents on the neighbouring village of Fallin. It was built to house the miners and their families who came to work in the coal pits sunk at Fallin in 1904. Today it must rate as one of the most unattractive depressed former mining villages in the country.

Across on the other shore the River Devon adds its waters to the Forth. Quarter of a mile upstream is the little village of Cambus or 'Cambus Pow' as it used to be known. 'Pow' is a Lowland corruption of the Gaelic *Pol*, meaning a sluggish backwater and this stretch of river used to provide a safe berth for the sailing ships which put in here to bring cargoes of barley to the village's two distilleries and sail out again with their holds tight packed with barrels of Scotch. Whisky was first distilled at Cambus in 1806, but as with so many other small Scottish distilleries all production has long since ceased and United Distillers operate the site simply as a vast sprawling bonded store to which a never ending stream of huge road tankers bring their loads to add to Scotland's ever increasing 'whisky loch'. Signs everywhere insist all visitors must report to the gate house, but there is little to see beyond the ugly security fences and the blank barred doors of the bonds, which sadly do not seem to possess the secret of how to persuade drinkers to return to their native tipple, rather than the increasingly popular lighter white spirits.

Round the corner past the local transport yard, whose heavy lorries add still further to the congestion, the Old Inn retains its charm and is a pleasant place to help use up some of that whisky by enjoying a dram, before continuing the walk downstream. Next door is the village Post Office, which an old guide book describes as offering telegraphic, money order and savings bank departments as well as four deliveries and dispatches every week day. The mail no doubt arrived and departed through Cambus Station, which also served Tullibody, three quarters of a mile inland, and offered return fares to Stirling at a cost of ten pence for first class and only four pence ha'penny for third class.

In the opposite direction by rail to Alloa was only two miles, but today the trains never come and so the choice is to drive into town past pleasant playing fields or to take the rougher route and walk beside the river as it loops to the south. Tucked in the bend is the first of the Forth islands of any size, Tullibody Inch. *Inch* is Gaelic for island and occurs again, more famously, once the river becomes the firth, in the names of Inchkeith, Inchcolm and Inchgarvie. Tullibody Inch does not seem to know whether it is inland, rural or coastal as a confusion of peewits and seagulls swirls overhead. The island is flat and marshy and on the shore of the river the fields are equally low lying. At places indeed they look as if they are below the level of the river and survive Dutch like only thanks to a rough rubble dyke. It is around this point the river water becomes salt and tidal.

Ahead lies the Rhind Peninsula along whose length used to run the railway line, carried across the river by the old Alloa Railway Bridge. Proposals to bridge the Forth at this point, where it is only quarter of a mile wide, were first put forward in 1817. It was not until 1879, however, that an Act of Parliament was passed empowering the construction of a new railway from the South Alloa branch on the south shore to Alloa on the north bank by means of a lattice girder bridge, The authorised capital expenditure was £60,000 of which the Caledonian Railway Company put up two thirds of the total as the new bridge would allow it to connect its lines to the south with its services in Fife, at a time before the construction of the more famous Forth Bridge at Queensferry.

Work on the Alloa Railway Bridge began in 1880 and when it was completed it enjoyed for a decade the honour of being the furthest point down stream that the Forth was bridged, until the Forth Bridge came into service in March 1890. The Alloa bridge was 570 yards long and seventeen feet wide on the outside of the girders. Inside the metal walls of the girders there was a width of fourteen feet, but although this would have allowed enough space for two lines only a single track was laid. The bridge was carried over the river by seventeen spans, two of 100 feet, two 80 feet and thirteen 68 feet long. Above the fairway of the channel, two of the 68 foot spans were designed to open each giving a clearance of sixty feet, for vessels to sail through. These movable spans swung on a massive central pier consisting of six cylindrical columns, manufactured by the engineering works of Watt and Wilson in Glasgow. All of this extra expense was necessary because of the Admiralty munitions depot at The Throsk, just up river on the south shore, to which it was considered much safer to transport explosives by river than overland by road. Today only the pillars, which carried the girders across the river, still stand, rising to a height of twenty four feet above high water mark and without walking the whole length of the Rhind Peninsula, are best seen from the south shore.

Taking the short cut across the neck of the Rhind the views at first remain rural with views of the second of the Forth Islands, Alloa Inch to be enjoyed, but closer to Alloa become increasingly, depressingly urban and it is necessary to make an inland detour to pass the factories of Weir Pumps and United Glass. Immediately past the latter the Earl of Mar's small boatyard provides a last vestige of activity at what was once the bustling port of Alloa. It is based around the pier constructed by the glass works to replace the old ferry pier, which its sprawling site enveloped. Across the river the remains of the ferry pier at South Alloa can just be glimpsed. Throughout Victorian times a small steam ferry plied to and fro between the two and the passage was maintained right up until the outbreak of the Second World War. During the 1930s the ferry was run by Alloa fishmongers, the Bremners, and there were enough passengers to keep three boats running every day.

As well as being ferrymen and fishmongers, the Bremners were also fishermen. They owned the rights to the salmon fishing between the old railway bridge upstream and Kennet Pans to the east and at one time enjoyed average weekly catches of around one thousand gleaming silver salmon.

Today such glittering riches and the activity needed to reap them are hard to imagine down by the riverside at Alloa. For Alloa seems to have turned its back on the Forth and forgotten its proud river heritage. All the signs of the old port with it prosperous dock and busy little harbour have been obliterated by infilling. A high security fence bars the way to the last rotting timbers of the wharfs and apart from a sewage works a little way further along the shore, the sites created by filling in the dock and harbour lie desolate and as unwanted as the port area itself became after the British Transport Commission closed it to navigation in 1961. That date is significant because if the dock at Alloa had survived for just another couple of decades into the 1980s it would no doubt have been turned into a visitor attraction with pleasant riverside walks providing views of its massive curved wooden dock gates and other items of industrial archaeology. Back in the sixties, however, such opportunities were missed and now on the walk down to what was formerly the port, even the old Ship Inn stands shuttered and the whole area has the feel that this, as far as Alloa is concerned, is definitely the wrong side of the tracks.

Yet it was once so very different as Alloa thrived on its river trade and the port was the heart of the town. 'A merchant of Alloa may trade to all parts of the world.' So wrote the author of *Robinson Crusoe*, Daniel Defoe in the diary of his tour of Scotland shortly before the Union of the Parliaments in 1707, when it is alleged he was actually spying for the English government. Looking at Alloa's now derelict harbour area it is difficult to realise that in Defoe's day more than one hundred sailing ships were registered here, so perhaps there really was something worth reporting back to his London paymasters.

With its view of green fields Alloa harbour seems far too far inland ever to have been the home of actual sea-going ships, but it was in fact its position far up the Forth right in the heart of central Scotland, which in the 18th century gave Alloa its original advantage. In those days Scotland's roads scarcely justified the name, being but muddy quagmires in winter and rutted dust bowls in summer and so the farther inland cargoes could be transported by water the better.

The middle of the 18th century was when the merchants of Glasgow were making their fortunes importing large quantities of tobacco from the American colonies. Most of the tobacco was imported through the River Clyde, but most of the profit came from its re-export to Holland and the other countries of Europe which could not buy direct from Virginia and the other British colonies in America because of the Navigation Laws. To protect and encourage British merchant shipping, so that the vessels could be requisitioned by the Royal navy in time of war, these laws stated that all colonial produce had to be trans-shipped through Britain. With this the Glasgow merchants complied by landing the tobacco at Clyde ports such as Greenock and Port Glasgow and they were quick to spot the advantages of Alloa as the nearest east coast port for its re-export to the continent.

Packhorse trains carried bales of tobacco overland from the Clyde to Alloa, where some of it was manufactured into cigars and snuff, but most was loaded straight onto sailing ships waiting in the harbour and carried to the Low Countries, where the Dutch preferred to process it for themselves.

From 1783 onwards, however, the Dutch cigarmakers could buy direct from the American growers because the Treaty of Paris which ended the War of Independence set the Colonists free. Thus almost overnight Alloa lost this element of its trade. Even worse, Alloa's old link with Glasgow suffered a second blow when in 1790 Scotland's first canal, the Forth and Clyde, provided the city with a direct water link with the new port of Grangemouth, which grew up rapidly where the canal joined the Forth.

Fortunately for Alloa, however, it had also become a centre for brewing and beer which in turn brought glass making to produce the bottles in which to sell it and both these industries kept the town's harbour busy with cargoes of grain and sand. Both industries have survived to this day, long after the harbour has been forgotten and the glass works have successfully diversified to compensate for the decline in demand for bottles as more beer is sold in cans.

In the middle of the 19th century Alloa as a port received a tremendous boost through the steady increase in the import of wooden pit-props for use in the area's coal industry. So large was this new trade that in 1861 it was decided to build a large new dock basin. When it was completed two years later it was 450 feet long, 137 feet broad and 24 feet deep with a 50 foot wide dock gate at its entrance from the river. At the same time a dry dock for ship repairs was also constructed and there was also a ship building yard, operated by the Grangemouth Dock Yard Company.

Alloa remained a prosperous port until the opening of Kincardine Bridge in 1936. As the world's largest swing bridge Kincardine in no way impeded ships reaching Alloa, but it so improved road transport from Grangemouth that it became faster for ships to discharge there and for their cargoes to be brought by road to Alloa's factories, than for the vessels to navigate the shallows to the town's own dock.

The Second World War brought a temporary reprieve for Alloa with the building of many MTB, motor torpedo boats and other small naval vessels at its dock. After peace returned in 1945 efforts were made to modernise the port, including electrification of the dock gates, but apart from occasional specialised cargoes it still could not compete with Grangemouth and so at the beginning of the 1960s the British Transport Commission officially closed Alloa as a port.

As well as the harbour and dock at Alloa, there were also good port facilities immediately across the river at South Alloa, which also had a flourishing pit-prop trade until the 1950s. Globe Petroleum also developed a small oil terminal at South Alloa and small tankers continued to dock there until into the 1980s.

CHAPTER 5
DUNMORE PINEAPPLE AND SALMON

From the industrial archaeology of South Alloa, which once even had its own direct railway line to Glasgow via Larbert it is pleasant to wander on along the south shore of the river to discover the rural peace and tranquillity of the lovely little village of Dunmore. Appearances can be deceptive however, because, while tiny Dunmore is today a placid backwater, it used once to thrive with not just one but three local industries.

A couple of black painted wooden keeled cobbles still lie in Dunmore's snug wee harbour or 'pool' as it is known locally, a last link with the fact that it used to be the centre of the Forth salmon industry. The salmon season ran from February to August with July the peak month. This doved in beautifully with harvesting on the surrounding farms and so the fishermen managed to keep themselves gainfully employed most of the year.

The method of fishing used at Dunmore was particularly interesting. It was known as 'hauf netting'. This meant that one end of the net was paid out over the stern of the cobble, while the other end of the net was walked along the shore, meaning there was little chance of escape for any salmon which swam into this net barrier.

As well as being famous for its salmon, Dunmore was also formerly well-known for its pottery. Pieces of Dunmore ware are now very collectable and a few are on display at the Pottery Inn, which is situated a little inland from the village.

Before hastening off to admire the pottery, or enjoy a drink, or both, notice the harbourside smiddy or blacksmith's forge. It is now over forty years since the last horses were shod here, but a reminder of these busier days is the smiddy's unusual doorway, shaped like an up turned horse shoe.

While Dunmore's industries have declined the rest of the village has been maintained in immaculate condition, providing an excellent example of one of Scotland's first model villages as they were known. For the whole of Dunmore was carefully planned and built during Victorian times by Catherine, Countess of Dundonald, to

The blacksmith's smiddy overlooks the mud-silted creek at Dunmore. John Doherty.

provide what were by the standards of the time, ideal living conditions for her estate workers and their families. Countess Catherine spent much of her time south of the border and perhaps this explains why her Scottish workers found themselves living in a distinctly English style hamlet, complete with diamond paned, latticed windowed cottages, set neatly round a village green.

But while the anglicised tastes of the countess influenced the style of housing at Dunmore, they could not affect the villagers' choice of sport and so, instead of cricket on the village green, it has always been games of bowls which have been played there and the bowling club still flourishes.

Whether Countess Catherine approved their choice of sport is not recorded, but she did thoughtfully provide for any players who felt thirsty, by providing a drinking fountain. The fountain, which was brought all the way from London, still stands in the middle of the green, but today it fails to live up to the message inscribed on it, which reads; 'Here quench your thirst and mark in me, an emblem of true charity, who while my bounty I restore, am neither heard or seen to flow. Repaid by fresh supplies from Heaven, for every cup of water given'.

Most notable feature of Countess Catherine's estate is the famous Dunmore Pineapple, constructed by her ancestor the Earl of Dundonald in 1761. In the 18th century the exotic, tropical pineapple was considered the symbol of hospitality and wrought iron pineapples from this period can still be found atop the black painted railings in front of many of Edinburgh's New Town houses and as far away as homes in America's colonial Williamsburg.

With coal both cheap and readily available from their own mines and pits, Scottish landowners vied with each other to produce tropical fruits in the huge hothouses, without which no walled garden was considered complete. Peaches, melons and grapes were all grown but the piece de resistance, to truly impress estate guests, was definitely the pineapple. The Earl of Dundonald therefore decided to go one better and top his greenhouses with a gigantic stone pineapple, which he could show off to his visitors all year round. And so the forty five foot (fifteen metre) high pineapple was constructed as the focal point of the sixteen acre walled garden. In the Earl's day the rooms in the Pineapple served as a garden retreat for his family and guests were entertained at summer tea parties. Now the Dunmore Pineapple still offers hospitality because it has been converted into what must be one of Britain's most unusual holiday homes, which can be rented from the Landmark Trust. The exterior of the pineapple is cared for by the National Trust for Scotland and members and other visitors are welcome to view this most unusual folly from the outside, all year round.

Returning to the riverbank, before leaving Dunmore, it is interesting to recall another curiosity, that it was here that Britain's furthest inland naval battle was fought. It took place just over two hundred years ago, when during the second Jacobite Rebellion in 1745 some of Prince Charles Edward Stuart's supporters managed to seize several small cannon, which they set up on the shore of the Forth at Dunmore. News of this reached Edinburgh, which was still in government hands and orders were given for a naval vessel to sail upriver to dislodge the rebels. This must have seemed an easy mission, but the captain and crew of the naval vessel were soon disillusioned, because the Jacobites put up a stubborn resistance. All day the calm of the Stirlingshire countryside was shattered by the steady exchange of shots between the shore battery and the ship. In the end the navy was forced to sail away without having defeated the Jacobites, but on the way back down river the naval captain vented his anger by destroying every boat he spotted along the south shore on the pretext of preventing them falling into enemy hands.

If a naval battle so far up the Forth may seem incongruous, it is worth remembering that Scotland's Royal Naval dockyard used to be situated just along the riverside in neighbouring Airth. During the middle ages timber was essential for ship building and the ready availability of plenty of wood made Airth an ideal choice for the construction of these early vessels for the infant Scottish navy, started by King James IV at the end of the 15th century. Ship building continued in Airth until the 18th century, but now all traces of the dockyard have disappeared and only a few carved sailing ships anchored securely to the stone lintels of some of Airth's historic homes are a reminder of the little town's former links with the sea.

Airth does however have several other items of historic interest, which make a detour off the Stirling to Grangemouth road well worth while. For tucked away behind the main street are several attractive 18th-century townhouses clustered round the mercat cross. This scene was at one time very familiar to television viewers because it was featured every week in the opening shots of Scotland's first ever soap opera, STV's *Garnock Way*.

The weather beaten stone market cross on which the TV cameras used to focus, bears the coats of arms of the two prominent local landowning families, the Bruces and the Elphinstones. It was erected as long ago as 1697, but Airth's much older original market cross can still also be found in a field at the top of the hill behind the village. The remains of this much earlier cross act as a reminder that the village of Airth first grew up on the crest of the hill, which is still dominated by the impressive castle of Fergus de Erth from whom it took its name.

Now a luxury country house hotel, Airth Castle's main claim to fame is the legend that it was there that Sir William Wallace performed one of his most daring feats of strength. During his time the castle had fallen into the hands of the enemy English and to make matters worse they used it as a prison in which they kept captive the Scottish patriot's uncle. Wallace vowed to revenge his family's honour by setting free his uncle and so with only a handful

The Dunmore Pineapple. Forth Valley Tourist Authority.

of followers, he crept across the rolling plain to the east of the castle, climbed silently up the steep hill and was so successful in his surprise raid that his band were able to storm the castle and kill all one hundred soldiers of the English Garrison.

Later Airth Castle came into the possession of the Graham family and during the 18th century they added the beautiful balconied entrance hall and the gracefully proportioned rooms which turned this ancient fortress into a stately Georgian mansion. Now Airth Castle Hotel also utilises the outbuildings of the estate's home farm and these have been attractively restored to form an unusual circular function suite, which amongst other events is ideal far larger wedding parties.

Wedding ceremonies themselves once took place at the castle because its grounds were the site for Airth's original parish church and the ruins can still be seen. They are surrounded by the graveyard and amongst the many interesting tombstones is one carved with this verse; 'Though winds and seas full forty years, have tossed me to and fro, in spite of these, by God's decrees, I'm anchored safe below'.

Perhaps this epitaph should act as a reminder to descend from the hill, return to the river and continue the journey downstream by crossing to the Clackmannan shore to discover what items of interest lie there.

CHAPTER 6

KENNET PANS TO KINCARDINE

As well as his huge estate at Dunmore, Lord Dundonald also had many interests across the Forth in Clackmannanshire including many coal pits. Dundonald was the leading Scottish colliery owner in the 17th-century campaign to end the serfdom amongst the miners, which for generations had thirled or legally bound them to work at the pit where they were born. Lord Dundonald argued that setting the miners free would make them better workers. He also reasoned that emancipating the miners was the only way to encourage other workers to come to work in the coal pits, where there was a growing demand for labour as a result of the growth of the industrial revolution. His enlightened views were not shared by many of his rival pit owners, but at last in 1774 parliament passed a law forbidding the thirling of miners to their pits, but those already tied to the mines were not granted their freedom straight away and it was not until 1799 that a second act declared that, 'all the colliers in that part of Great Britain called Scotland are hereby declared to be free from their servitude'.

Having set his miners free, Lord Dundonald did, however, still show a great paternalistic interest in them. Nowhere was this better seen than in the miners' rows, the long low lines of miners' homes at Kennet Pans. In particular his lordship was proud of the savings scheme which he introduced and which proved so successful that, 'the miners are able to provide themselves with good clothes and household furniture and to lay in a supply of beef for their families in November. Indeed they have carried the taste for the elegantariorum of life further than many may think necessary; most of them have silver watches, clocks in all their homes and on Sundays wear silk stockings, tambour embroidered silk vests and have their hair well dressed and powdered'. The Alloa parish minister shared his view noting how neat and well dressed the miners and their wives had become on Sundays. Lord Dundonald also tried to ensure that the Miners' children all went to school and in 1780 bought thirteen cows to ensure all of them received fresh milk each day.

One of the main reasons for the success of the pits at Kennet Pans was the ease with which the coal could be exported through the little port. Its other cargo was whisky from the village's own distillery and from the nearby Kilbagie Distillery, which it is interesting to note was exported duty free. In 1733 Kennetpans was the largest distillery in Scotland. Its workforce included the five Haig brothers, whose name was to become famous. As well as being shipped, some of the whisky was of course also consumed locally and unfortunately its ready availability led some of the local folk to appear in the burgh court at nearby Clackmannan Tolbooth. Today only the bell tower of the old Tolbooth remains standing, but when it was originally built in 1592 at a cost of £284 it also included the court room, jailer's house and prison. Not all wrong doers however were lucky enough to escape with a fine or a spell in the cells. For the Clackmannan magistrates also believed in the persuasive powers of the long leather lash and the local market cross still bears the marks of the chains, which bound culprits to its stone column during their public flogging.

The view from Clackmannan is dominated by its tower which from 1365 to 1772 was the home of the Bruce family. Its hilltop site is a good place to heed Clackmannanshire's old motto, 'Look Aboot Ye' and doing just that it is possible to take in at a glance most of what was always taught in school to be Scotland's smallest county, with the longest name. Back, up river to the west, the windings of the infant Forth can be clearly seen but ahead to the east it has matured and the river now flows fast and free towards the sea.

In the immediate forefront it's as if the Forth's coming of age is appropriately marked by its flowing below the 'Silver Link' as the Kincardine on Forth Road Bridge was affectionately nicknamed when it was first opened in 1936. At the time it was the lowest point on the river's course at which it was bridged and people on both shores were particularly proud of the fact that this feat had been achieved by the construction of the world's longest swing bridge. This record is still held by Kincardine because although it last swung open in the 1980s and will never do so again, its 364 foot long central swing span has never been equalled.

Not only is Kincardine a world record holder, it can also claim to have operated faultlessly throughout over five decades, a fine tribute indeed to the skill of its designer, J Guthrie Brown CBE, of the Edinburgh engineering firm, Sir Alexander Gibb and Company.

Throughout the fifty years of its working life, until it was officially declared a static structure, Kincardine was manned round the clock by a ten man crew. Standing at the controls, high above the road deck, felt exactly like being on the bridge of an ocean liner as its operation was controlled by a ship's wheel. When it first came into use in 1936 it took almost half an hour to open to allow a vessel to sail through, but over the years a lot of careful thought and practice by the bridge master and his men reduced this time to only eleven minutes and on one record breaking occasion to ten. Equally amazingly each opening cost less than 5p in electricity. The reason for this was that once the bridge was set in motion it was carried through its swing by its own momentum.

Each opening was co-ordinated from the control room and there was a careful series of safety checks from the moment when the traffic lights changed to amber then red, right through until when the portcullis like gates at either end of the swing span were raised and the traffic flowed again, to ensure that no vehicle was trapped or any way endangered. From the outset Kincardine was equipped with the very latest scientific aids and was the first place in Scotland equipped with photo-electric cells, which controlled the return to position of the bolts and wedges, which locked the central span to the north and south ends after each manoeuvre. As the swing span dropped two inches when it was opened the photo electric cells were vital to ensure the road surface had been raised again and was exactly in line and absolutely level, before the connecting bolts were rammed home.

Motorists crossing Kincardine were often intrigued by the series of posts stuck in the mud on the south shore. The reason for them was that the southern end of the bridge is situated on the Central Scotland geographic fault line and there was no bed rock on which to site the piers. Regular readings had therefore to be taken to record any changes in the level of the south bank and the poles in the mud formed the base line for these geometric exercises.

Over the years the records also showed that any land reclamation even as far down river as Bo'ness could have an effect on the tides, which swirl past the bridge piers at six to seven knots and a concrete breakwater was constructed on the south shore to provide protection. Another measure designed to minimise wear and tear was that every week opposite ends of the swing span

When Kincardine Bridge came into use in 1936, it was the furthest point downstream that the Forth could be crossed by road. It is still the longest swing bridge in the world, although its central span is now never opened for ships to sail through. W F Hendrie.

were positioned at the north and south ends of the bridge. To achieve this Kincardine was closed at 6 am every Sunday morning, which was the quietest time of the week for traffic, and the swing span was swung through half a revolution. This service opening was also utilised for maintenance purposes such as greasing. The bridge's engine room situated under the road deck in the middle of the river was in fact so carefully looked after that not a single item of moving machinery ever had to be replaced during its whole operational life.

The bridge engineers were also responsible for the smooth operation of the north and south portcullis gates, which had to be lowered and raised at each opening to seal off the swing span. They were also in charge of the bridge's emergency equipment, which included its own fire tender and a life boat, both of which were situated down on the wood planked deck of the central pier. Most emergencies however happened when vehicles broke down on the bridge. Unlike the original policy when the Forth Road Bridge first opened in 1964 drivers who were unfortunate enough to break down on Kincardine were never fined or charged for the removal of their vehicle. The policy was that the main thing was to remove the obstruction with least delay. Ice and snow were another problem both on the road surface and on the super-structure and over the years spraying with a variety of de-icing solutions were tried of which pigs' urine was found most effective if it had not been for the dreadful smell!

Kincardine's safe operation was the responsibility of the Scottish Development Department's Road Division whose officials were responsible for all of Scotland's major road bridges. All agreed, however, that none had quite the character of half-mile long Kincardine. It was a feeling perhaps best summed up by Kincardine's bridge master, George Reid, who often claimed that he and his crew looked upon the bridge as 'very much alive' and described its opening as, 'like Hampden Park football pitch turning round on a central pivot'.

Before the construction of Kincardine a ferry used to ply across the river to Higginsneuk. There the Keith Arms Inn where travellers used to enjoy a refreshment while waiting for the boat to make the crossing still serves drinks by the riverside. It is called the Keith Arms, because the site it stands on used to be Admiral Lord Keith of Tulliallan's only land on the south shore of the Forth. Nearby on the southern approach road to the bridge is the very 1930s looking Silver Link Roadhouse. Its style of architecture and name are both a reminder of how this stretch of coast changed dramatically with the opening of the bridge in 1936, a date recorded permanently on the commemorative stone on the south archway along with the Stirlingshire coat of arms. It is paralleled on the facade of the northern arch with the Clackmannanshire armorial bearings complete with the former county's motto, 'Look aboot ye'.

Doing just that and looking out over Kincardine, the skyline of the little town is incongruously dominated by two tower blocks of hideous 1960s flats. Walk down into its streets, however and it's possible to find over sixty of its 18th-century buildings with features such as the red pantiled roofs, harled walls and foresteps, which have made neighbouring Culross such a tourist attraction. In contrast Kincardine has a rather neglected look about it from the disused electricity generating station, superseded by the giant Longannet further along the coast, to its once busy piers now deserted apart from one or two fishing boats. Yet at one time Kincardine had its own shipbuilding yard and the salt pans from which it took its original name of Newpans. Today it is best known as the site of the police training college for the whole of Scotland at nearby Tulliallan Castle and for its two industries, coal mining to provide fuel for Longannet and papermaking at Kilbagie Mills, now part of the Inveresk Group.

CHAPTER 7

CULROSS, PRONOUNCED CURRUS

While Kincardine has been allowed to develop and decline just like any other small Scottish town its near neighbour, Culross is as if it has been preserved in a time warp. It's situated only three miles further along the Fife shore, but entering it is like travelling back three hundred years through history.

Three centuries ago Culross was one of Scotland's most prosperous royal burghs, its little harbour bustling with sailing ships loading cargoes of locally produced coal and salt for export and unloading cargoes ranging from iron to the finest cloths and from the richest spices to the bright red pantiles, which can still be seen on the roofs of the town's homes.

Then the fortunes of Culross changed and it began to decline for a variety of reasons from the decrease in the demand for sea salt to the increase in mud in the harbour and from the fall in coal production to the rise in size of ships, which became too big to berth in its tiny port.

And so from the beginning of the 18th century to the start of the 20th century Culross slumbered in a sleep, even longer than Sleeping Beauty's. The kiss which brought it back to life came just over sixty years ago in 1932, not from a handsome prince, but from the newly formed Scottish National Trust, which acquired many of the town's houses as its first ever purchase.

Fortunately unlike so many American ghost towns, the Trust decided from the outset that it did not want to preserve Culross in aspic jelly as some kind of museum, but determined to bring it back to life. This is did by restoring many of what have become known as The Little Houses and then offering them at economic rents so many young families moved back into the old burgh. With the taste, which has been the hall mark of the Scottish National Trust in all its developments in over six decades since then, the restoration of The Little Houses was painstakingly carried out using only the best of Scottish craftsmanship and traditional materials, so that externally they look exactly as they must have done in the sixteen hundreds, while indoors they have been carefully modified to make comfortable modern homes. One of The Little Houses has even been cunningly utilised to accommodate the town's electricity sub power station, thus ensuring nothing modern intrudes on the historic scene.

As private homes The Little Houses are not open to visitors and can only be viewed from the streets, but the Trust does have several properties where it is possible to go indoors to relive the past. Its headquarters is in the quaint thick stone walled Town House, whose curved Dutch belfry is a constant reminder of the trade which once flourished between Culross and the Low Countries on the continent, long before the European Community was ever thought of. The old Town House dominates the town green or Sandhaven as it is called, just as it dominated life in the 17th-century burgh. Here can still be seen the tron, where goods were weighed when they were unloaded in the harbour, although the river is now more distant because of land reclamation and cut off, because of the single track railway line which divides it from the shore.

Climb the unusual double sided stairway and you enter the wood panelled council chamber, where the Town Councillors of Culross met weekly from its creation as a Royal Burgh in 1588 until the reorganisation of Scottish local government following the Wheatley Report in 1975 robbed towns of their independence. Rather than see their historic meeting place taken over by Fife Regional Council, the last piece of business transacted by the Culross councillors at their final meeting was to hand over their Town House to the safe keeping of the National Trust. The Trust could not have found a more appropriate headquarters because the Town House is alive with history from the decisions taken at the council meetings to the sentences passed at the weekly burgh court and including the stories of the Culross witches who were once imprisoned there in special attic cells, as it was feared that if they were held captive in the usual basement ones they might commune with the Devil. Now these and other Culross stories are told in the Town House's audio visual show, while actual artefacts such as the famous Culross weights and measures help bring the past still further to life. The Culross Chaldron was accepted as the standard coal measure throughout Scotland.

Just as the Trust's headquarters in Culross is particularly suitable, so too is the home of its representative in the town, who

The Town House at Culross is now the National Trust for Scotland's Visitor Centre, with an excellently concise audio-visual display about the Burgh's varied past. Notice the curved Dutch-style belfrey, and, to either side of the foot of the tower, the tiny windows of the attic cells, where witches were imprisoned. Dr Arthur Down.

occupies the well-known and very distinctive turreted house, always known as The Study. The Study takes its unusual name from the fact that it was used for several years as a study and reading room by Bishop Leighton of Culross Abbey. It later became the home of one of the burgh's many wealthy merchants and it is as such that it is now furnished with a painted wooden kist from Norway, blue and white Dutch tiles round the fireplace and at the very top of the spiral stair the little lookout room is still lined with solid Baltic pine.

High above America's historic Hudson River in upper new York State the Rockefellar family's mansion is called Kykuit, meaning Look Out, because their sprawling hillside estate was originally farmed by the same Dutch settlers, who originally called New

York, New Amsterdam. Say Kykuit with a Scottish accent and you can indeed 'keek oot', if you are one of the small groups of visitors allowed to climb to the top of the spiral stair, so steep there's a rope to help haul you up. Staring out of the tiny window, it is not difficult to imagine you are the merchant scanning the Forth for a first glimpse of a home coming ship, just like Shakespeare's Antonio on the Rialto in distant Venice.

Like Antonio and his fellow merchants of Venice, the merchants of Culross were eager to maximise their profits. On outward voyages to the Scandinavian countries, Germany and the Scottish staple at De Veere, the holds of their little sailing ships were always brim full of coal and salt. With the profits from these their skippers, which is of course another Dutch word, bought fine Flanders cloth and the pepper, nutmeg, cinnamon and other spices brought to the Netherlands by the famous Dutch East India Company. Such luxuries were much in demand in Scotland to make fashionable dresses for the richest of ladies and to add flavour to the Scottish diet, but they came in such small quantities they could be easily stowed in the sea chest in the captain's cabin. This gave rise to the old Scottish saying, 'Guid gear gaes in sma' bulk', but though true, this also left the skippers with a problem. For it meant the holds of their ships were empty. Ships without cargo are known as 'light', which means they ride high out of the water and are thus prime targets for the vicious North Sea gales which so often whip this shallow water into a witch's cauldron of stomach churning waves. Rather than risk what would now no doubt be described as a 'white knuckle ride home' the masters of the sailing ships therefore wisely filled their holds with heavy cargoes, those readily available being made up of Dutch clay roofing pantiles, decorative blue and white delft tiles and loads of iron. Thus they earned the gratitude of their crew by reducing the likelihood of sea sickness and of their Culross owners by increasing their profits from this extra cargo.

Once unloaded the red pantiles were used to roof local homes and evidence of this can still be seen in coastal towns on both sides of the Forth, while as already described in The Study the other tiles were used for interior decoration. This left the iron, whose availability led to another industry for which Culross be-came well-known, because the local blacksmiths or 'Hammermen' as they were known and described in the burgh's coat of arms, turned it into girdles. These girdles were not an iron version of the corsetry used by twentieth-century ladies to control wayward figures, but the flat iron pans used to bake the scones and pancakes or drop scones, which may have given their figures problems in the first place. Culross girdles were so well made that King James VI and I rewarded the 'hammermen' with a royal monopoly stating they alone in the whole of Scotland were allowed to manufacture these kitchen utensils. That the royal warrant was appreciated and valued may be seen from the fact that when black-smiths in the neighbouring village of Valleyfield only two miles further down river, chanced their hands at producing girdles, the 'hammermen' immediately invoked the king's sanction and Culross retained its monopoly. This monopoly led to an old Scottish saying, which was feared by generations of bairns. For if a wean stepped out of line its mother would shout, 'I'll mak' yer lug ding like a Culross girdle', and if the misbehaviour did not cease no doubt followed up their threat with an actual clout round the ear.

Today the Culross 'hammermen' are still remembered on the burgh's coat of arms displayed on the lamps of the street lights at the Town House and examples of the black iron girdles which they made may be seen by the hearths in both The Study and The Palace. The Palace is the National Trust's main visitor attraction in Culross. It was originally built in 1597 by the burgh's richest merchant Sir George Bruce. How it got its name is not certain. Perhaps it was so large and impressive compared to the surrounding Little Houses that the local folk gave it this title as a nickname. On the other hand, perhaps it was originally simply Sir George Bruce's place and bad spelling changed it into The Palace.

No matter which, The Palace is definitely well worth exploring as it has many unusual features. Entering the walled garden the original building of The Palace stands on the left. The room which juts out was the guest chamber, dating back to the middle ages when there were very few inns, but rich local home owners maintained the old monastic tradition of providing travellers with free overnight accommodation. The room's outside door leading to the little separate flight of forestairs in front of the building, meant overnight guests could make an early morning start to their journeys without disturbing the still sleeping host family.

For family guests, several of the bedrooms had ornately painted

The Little Houses, restored by the National Trust for Scotland, are one of Culross's best-known features. Dr Arthur Down.

ceilings, several of which have been restored to their full colour glory. Most impressive, however, of the rooms in the Palace is the vaulted chamber with its curved wood panelled ceiling. This fine room must indeed have given great pride to Sir George, especially as just to the left at the fire place end is one of Scotland's first indoor lavatories. Downstairs the stone flagged kitchen was also considered most modern, because it had a system of running water. How it worked can still be traced. How Sir George was able to afford all of these touches, which in his day must have been considered so luxurious, is explained in the upstairs counting house, where his fortune was kept safe by the iron door and brick floor, which was a protection against fire.

Sir George made his money from two sources, salt and coal and it was his production of the latter which resulted in a royal visit to the Palace. The reason for this was that one of his collieries was considered a wonder of the age. This was the Moat Pit, which was so cunningly designed that the shaft came up in the middle of the Forth out in Culross Bay. The benefit of this was that it meant loads of coal could be delivered straight into the holds of the waiting sailing ships, thus avoiding completely the necessity for any form of land transport, which was slow, difficult and most importantly very costly. To construct the Moat Pit, Sir George chose a site just under 400 metres out in Culross Bay, directly opposite Castle Hill and St Serf's church on the shore. Work could take place only twice a day at low tide, but gradually an island began to take shape. Circular and roughly 20 metres in diameter, it was built completely of large blocks of stone. These were sealed together with thick black bituminous tar until the man made island was entirely water tight. In the centre a smaller circle six metres wide was left empty and it was there that Sir George ordered his miners to begin digging out what was to become the famous Moat Pit. Down and down they dug through the bed of the river until they hit coal. From this point deep below the Forth mining began and the workings were connected to the shore by a submarine tunnel.

The fame of this early 17th-century engineering feat soon spread, even apparently as far as the royal court in London, because when in 1617 King James VI and I made his first return visit to Scotland since he moved to the English capital following the Union of the Crowns, fourteen years earlier in 1603, he requested that he visit the Moat at Culross as part of his royal progress.

On the day of his arrival His Majesty was welcomed by Sir George and his wife and all of their children and entertained to a suitably lavish dinner. Next morning Sir George proudly conducted his royal guest underground and out below Culross bay through the submarine tunnel. Soon they reached the coal workings and the foot of the Moat shaft. After they had inspected the coal face Sir George invited His Majesty to climb to the top of the shaft for what should have been the highlight of the tour, the view across the Forth. But when King Jamie emerged into the daylight, he was apparently so surprised and startled to find himself entirely surrounded by water that he panicked. Fearing he was involved in yet another plot like the Gunpowder Plot, to assassinate him, he is said to have bawled, 'TREASON!'

So shaken was the King that he declined to return underground. Instead Sir George arranged for James to be rowed ashore by boat and together they walked from the harbour back to the Palace. His Majesty must apparently have forgiven Sir George because he knighted him. Just how proud Sir George was of this honour can still be seen to this day because on the facade of the newer block of The Palace, across the courtyard, are carved the initials SGB, Sir George Bruce.

As well as making money from coal, Sir George also maximised his profits by using the dross or panwood as it became known to fuel fires to produce salt by evaporating water from the river. The Scottish salt industry flourished for over three hundred years at various places where carboniferous coal measures outcropped on the coast, from Saltcoats in the west to Prestonpans in the east.

The method used was to set up a huge wooden see-saw like piece of equipment on the shore. On one end was a large wooden bucket and this the miners' wives and children, who made up most of the labour force at the pans, pushed down and under the surface of the river until it was full of salt water. The bucket was then pushed round until it was over the shore where it was tipped and emptied into a deep basin known as the reservoir. This procedure was meant to allow most of the silt and other impurities to settle to the bottom, before the water was finally transferred into the actual pan. The pans, which were raised off the ground on small stone pillars were oblong in shape approximately seven metres long and four metres wide.

Despite the use of the reservoir some impurities still remained in the water. Once it was boiling, therefore, a bucket of ox or sheep blood was emptied into it. The idea was that the albumen in the blood thickened, congealed and formed a scum, like that which forms when making strawberry jam. This scum floated to the surface carrying the impurities with it. It was then the women's unpleasant job to remove it. This they did by reaching out over the bubbling, boiling solution and scraping it off using wooden rakes, as these did not conduct the fierce heat and burn the women's hands as would have happened with ones made of iron.

The solution then boiled away round the clock by day and night until at last the water evaporated, leaving behind the spark-ling silver crystals of salt on the pan walls. It took fifty tons of coal to produce three tons of salt. The fires were never allowed to go out and their deep red glow was often used like an early form of light house by vessels navigating the river. The only time the fires beneath the pans were damped down was on Saturday nights. This was because the kirk session strictly forbade the production of any salt on Sundays. This delay was however turned to advantage by the wily salt masters because the reduced rate of evaporation resulted in larger grains of salt being formed and these were

The Palace, built by the most prosperous of the Culross merchants, Sir George Bruce. Red pantiles and crow-step gables are attractive features. The latter always led to chimneys and were a clever Scottish idea which allowed sweeps to climb up and clean lums from the outside rather than utilise the poor little chimney boys, as was the custom in England. Dr Arthur Down.

marketed as a more expensive table delicacy called Sabbath Salt.

Even the ordinary salt was considered too expensive by Scottish housewives, who objected strongly to the fact that the Privy Council taxed it as an essential commodity required by every family to salt away their winter supply of meat. After the salt was produced it was stored in locked warehouses called girnels and as in the case of whisky in bonded stores, custom and excise officers ensured tax was paid before it could be removed for sale in Scottish inland towns, which could not supply their own requirements for this essential commodity.

For many years the saltpan workers were paid in salt. To obtain money they sold their salt to the chapmen, who came chapping or knocking on their doors each week and swapped it either for cash or more usually for other goods which they required.

The Scottish salt industry suffered two major blows in the 18th century. The agrarian revolution resulted in the introduction of root vegetables such as turnips and mangolds which provided winter fodder, thus meaning that farm animals ·no longer had to be slaughtered each autumn and that beef, mutton and pork no longer had to be salted to last until the spring. Around the same time salt mines were developed in Cheshire and on the continent in Germany. Rock salt was of superior quality. For a time the Scottish salt manufacturers tried to combat the import of rock salt by mixing small quantities of it with their own product to improve its quality, but in the end by the beginning of this century sea salt was used only for non-edible purposes such as foot baths and clearing frost and snow from the roads in winter. Across the river from Culross the fire beneath the last of the thirteen pans in Bo'ness was finally allowed to go out in 1890, but down river at Joppa near Musselburgh and at Prestonpans the last pans did not close until the 1950s.

Back at Culross, a doocote, now cunningly converted to conceal the town's carpark toilets, is a last reminder of the days when squabs, fat young pigeons, were a welcome alternative to the usual winter diet of salt beef and mutton.

While all other traces of the old salt industry have disappeared from Culross, many other links with the burgh's historic past can still be seen by walking through its narrow streets. The streets are for instance still paved with the uneven stone setts or causies just as they have been for centuries past. Walk along the raised row of setts in the middle and you occupy what was known as the 'croon o' the causie'. In the past this was a privilege reserved for the bailies, magistrates, merchants and other important lieges as this meant they could keep their shoes and boots dry as they walked through the town. Bairns, servants and the poor were expected to know their place and keep well out of the way, by running along the gutters on either side.

Up the brae in the shadow of The Study, the stones of the mercat cross are every bit as ancient as those of the steep lanes which lead to it. Here too any of the town's youths or poor, who broke its rules were taught their lesson as the tall column of the cross doubled as the burgh's whipping post. Floggings with a leather lash were administered on market days to ensure the punishment also acted as a deterrent to the crowds, who flocked into the square to shop at the stalls, which surrounded it. The half shuttered windows, which can still be seen high on the walls of the surrounding buildings, provided an even better grandstand view of the scourgings and all the other activities of market days. The idea of the half shuttered windows was that when the earliest glass panes let light in, but were too thick to see through, the shutters beneath could be opened to see out.

While stalls were only put up on market days, evidence of one of the burgh's permanent businesses can also be found in the square with the sign for the butcher's shop carved in the wall near the forestairs, so called because they stood before or in front of the building. Notice also the tirling pins, the metal rings, which formed a novel alternative to door knockers. Further up the brae, on the opposite side, can be seen another old Culross business, the snuff shop with its 17th-century version of an advertising slogan for the rich, brown, aromatic tobacco snuff once produced there, 'Wha would a thocht it, noses would a bocht it'.

Someone who may well have done just that was perhaps the dominie, who taught in the school at the top of the hill opposite the abbey. The adjacent graveyard provides details on its tombstones of many of the other townsfolk who lived and worked in Culross, while in the entrance to the church, boards set high on the walls detail gifts given to the poor of the parish. Notice also the pewter offering plates with the old spelling of the town's name Curris inscribed upon them. Why this was later changed to Culross while the pronunciation remained unaltered is a mystery.

Culross Abbey is one of Scotland's most historic churches. According to local tradition it dates back as long ago as the 4th century when on his travels, St Serf came to where Bo'ness now stands on the opposite side of the Forth. There as he gazed out across the river legend has it that a sunbeam lit up the Fife shore. It is claimed that he took this to be a sign that it was there that he should establish his church and the ruins of the monastery, which

The Study, with its attic look-out windows, from which news of the town's home-bound merchant ships with their rich cargoes, could first be gathered. Dr Arthur Down.

grew up around it still stand on the hillside below the abbey.

Like most religious establishments Culross Abbey had its school. One of the pupils was a boy whose name was Kentigern and who was destined to become one of Scotland's most famous sons. He is said to have been the grandson of King Lothus from whom Lothian took its name and that he was born in Culross after his unmarried mother Princess Thametis fled the royal court, because she was expecting him. To escape her father's wrath, tradition has it that she escaped from the court at Traprain Law near Haddington and made her way to the coast of the Forth near North Berwick. There she found a small open rowing boat and put out into the river. For several days and nights she was exposed to the elements, but survived, until eventually the boat was swept ashore at Culross.

There, shortly afterwards she gave birth to the baby who was christened Kentigern. When he was old enough to go to the abbey school, he was apparently unpopular with the other pupils, because they felt that as a prince the monks gave him too many privileges. Each morning at dawn it was the duty of one of the boys to rekindle all of the lights and fires in the monastery from the one flame kept alive throughout the night. When it was Kentigern's turn, they put out the flame in the hope that unable to carry out his task he would at last be whipped by the master of discipline. Young Kentigern however escaped being beaten, because when he discovered the flame had been extinguished he simply rubbed a branch from a tree, which promptly blazed into fire. With this brand he quickly lit all of the flares and fires, much to the amazement of his disappointed classmates.

Later when he grew up Kentigern went on to impress many more people, because he travelled west until he reached the River Clyde and there, where Glasgow grew, he converted the populace to the Christian faith. There he also assumed a new name and is still remembered to the present day as Scotland's largest city's patron, St Mungo, a fact commemorated in the abbey by the inclusion of Glasgow's coat of arms in the stained glass window in the apse.

There are many other interesting features in the abbey. Look for the strikingly modern stained glass of the Bruce family window with its gold and scarlet saltire cross. The family's mansion house home stands on the outskirts of the town. At the other end of the nave in the north aisle is the marble tomb of the original Sir George and Lady Bruce, who King James VI and I honoured with a royal visit, and on the front are carved all eight sons and daughters of their large family.

On an adjacent wall there is an engraving of a human heart. The reason for its presence begins with the story of a duel. It was fought far away from Scotland in the little Dutch town of Bergen-op-Zoom in the year 1613. The two opponents were Edward, Lord Bruce, who had travelled there on business from Culross and the English Earl of Dorset, with whom he had quarrelled. The duel is described as having been, 'fierce and bloody' both combatants inflicting cuts on each other with their swords, before Bruce suffered a fatal blow and fell mortally wounded. With his dying breath he is said to have begged that his heart be cut out and taken home to be buried in Culross. So while his body was laid to rest in the great church of Bergen-op-Zoom, his heart was removed and shipped home to be buried in the abbey, where he had so often worshipped as a youth. Strangely at some point during the 18th century all trace of the heart was lost. In 1808, however, Sir Robert Preston of Valleyfield House, organised a search of the abbey and according to the plaque on the wall, the heart, 'was found embalmed in a silver case of foreign workmanship, secured between two flat and excavated stones, clasped with iron, and was again carefully replaced and securely deposited in the spot, where it was discovered'.

What the elders of the Culross kirk session thought of the fatal duel is not recorded, but as a court of the church they were certainly strict enough with their own congregation. In particular they were always on the alert for Sabbath breakers. In 1646 one George Anderson was reported to them, accused of Wee Willie Winkie like, 'running up and doone the toone', but instead of doing it at night to see, 'if all the bairns were in their beds', he foolishly did so, 'in tyme of Devine service'. Anderson confessed his sin and promised, 'never to doe the lyke here after', but the session was not satisfied because the elders discovered to their horror that his absence from the kirk had resulted in him, 'not knowing what commandment he had broken'. The session therefore enacted that, 'If he whould not get the commandments betwixt then and that day twenty days, he should be brought back and scourged publicly'. The thought of the lash stinging across his bare back, appears to have galvanised Anderson into committing the commandments to memory, because there is no record of the threatened whipping ever taking place.

Having caught and dealt with Anderson, the kirk session decided it must take action to deter any other parishioners from being tempted to copy his example and miss worship. The elders therefore decided that they must make the sacrifice of themselves missing the minister's sermon and that each Sunday several of them should patrol Culross to make certain all the other towns people were safely in the pews. On their first Sunday on duty the searchers, as they described themselves, did indeed have to take action, because they found several men gossiping in the Sandhaven in front of the Town House. Two of the women of the burgh, Christian Blyth and Janet Cunningham were both caught working in their gardens. They pled that they were not actually gardening, but had only ventured out, 'to pull a few sybows for their kail pots'. This excuse did not land them in the soup, because they were allowed off with a sharp rebuke.

That for the time being put an end to the adults 'stravaiging on the Sabath', but there was still the problem of the bairns. For the

Culross children were not only running about the streets, but were daring to play games down at the harbour, when they should have been sitting attentively in the abbey on the hill. The session met to consider this disgraceful behaviour and ordered that an act should be read from the pulpit on the following Lord's Day, forbidding boys and girls to play in the streets both before and after the sermon as well as during it.

Even in the 17th century there appear to have been juvenile delinquents because some time later the session had before it two laddies accused not only of playing on the Sabbath but of, 'making Bailie Pearson's son's horse shy and throw the bairn as he rode down from the church to the waterside'. One of the accused was James Hendrie! Perhaps fortunately, their punishment is not described.

Those who did conscientiously attend the kirk were not safe from the censure of the session. Several were punished by being made to sit on the cutty stool or seat of repentance for daring to fall asleep during the minister's sermon. Others were chided for making a noise while the children were saying their catechism.

Despite the strictness of the kirk elders, many of the people of Culross appear to have obstinately continued to believe in black magic and the building on the corner opposite the abbey is still known as The House of the Evil Eye, because the two small windows below its curved Dutch gable look just like eyes, which uncannily follow visitors as they walk past! Well-known Scottish children's author Kathleen Fiddler, after whom the annual national award for children's fiction is named, knew all about the superstitions of Culross and used it as the setting for her novel about witchcraft, *Escape In the Dark*. The House of the Evil Eye, the belfry of the abbey, the attic cells in the Town House and the Moat Pit all feature in her intriguing tale, which has over the years put Culross on the Scottish literary map for many younger readers.

CHAPTER 8
SKINFLATS TO CARRON

Over on the south shore of the river the first place after Kincardine Bridge is Skinflats. Skinflats gained fame when the well-known *Scotsman* diarist Wilfred Taylor one day in his column dubbed it the ugliest place name in Scotland. Skinflats, however, really means the entire opposite. For its name was given to it by the Dutch engineers, brought to Scotland in the 18th century to undertake an ambitious land reclamation scheme. Using all of the skills learned back home in the Low Countries the Dutchmen were successful in winning many acres from the Forth between Kincardine and Grangemouth. At first the flat lands which emerged from the river were too salt for agricultural use, but within a few years it was possible to sow grass. Looking out over the new green fields, their expertise had helped win from the river, the Dutch engineers were so proud of their achievement, that they called them the 'beautiful plains'. Unfortunately the local Scots could not pronounce the Dutch words and so they became corrupted to Skinflats as they are still known to this day. Even now, however, the little village does still have one last link with Holland and the foreign engineers, who came to stay and change the landscape, because its pub restaurant is still called the Dutch Inn.

Skinflats came back into the news in the early 1990s for the flat fields reclaimed by the Dutch are now those farmed by the Sutherland family, whose son Tom was unlucky enough to become one of the Beirut hostages. Professor Sutherland was working for the American University in Lebanon when he was captured. Throughout his ordeal his family in the farmhouse at Skinflats never gave up hope that he would be released and when he was finally freed he returned for a thanksgiving service in the old stone-built church at nearby Bothkennar, where he had worshiped as a boy.

Sadly the quiet living Sutherland family were again thrust into the full glare of the media spotlight only a year later when his sister Elizabeth died during the Scottish outbreak of Necrotising Fasciitis, the tragic flesh devouring disease, and her funeral service was held in the same little kirk.

So pancake flat is the surrounding countryside that the spire of Bothkennar Kirk can be seen for miles around and used to be used as a helpful landmark by the skippers of boats sailing up the Carron River, which is the next place of interest on the south shore. Today the Carron is very much silted up with mud and difficult even for small craft to navigate, but it is interesting to note that when the Old Pay Brig, which carried the road over the river between Skinflats and Glensburgh, was built, it was designed so that the central span could open to enable ships to sail through. This was very important because many vessels sailed up and down the Carron to Carronshore delivering raw materials for the world famous Carron Iron Works and sailing out again with the foundry's products.

The River Carron, from which the ironworks took their name, was in fact one of the most important reasons why this site was chosen for the construction of Scotland's first large scale foundry, because its 18th-century founders recognised the great importance of sea transport. At first the ironworks might well have been built much further down the Forth at Cockenzie in East Lothian, because a site there would also have had immediate access to the river and it was near the home of the Cadell family.

The Cadells were a prosperous family of Scottish merchants, who had made their wealth from the import of iron from the continent, especially Russia and Sweden, at a time when the production of iron in this country was still a very small scale rural industry with a tiny output. Just at the time when there was a profitable increase in the demand for the Cadell's imported iron thanks to the outbreak in 1756 of what later became known as the Seven Years War, the same hostilities interrupted the supply, because of the action of the enemy France against allied shipping. The Cadells were therefore anxious to set up a large scale foundry in Scotland and went into partnership with two English industrialists Samuel Garbett and Dr John Roebuck.

Born in 1718, Roebuck was the son of a prosperous Sheffield cutler. The Roebucks were originally a French Huguenot family. This family background meant that although Roebuck was very clever at school and his father's wealth could easily have paid the fees he was barred from going to either of the only two universities which existed in England at the time, Oxford and Cambridge, because of the Religious Test Acts, which decreed all students must

The Auld Pay Brig which carried the road over the Carron, between Skinflats and Glensburgh. Now most traffic speeds by over the bridge which carries the dual carriageways of the M9 Stirling to Edinburgh motorway across the river.

be communicant members of the Church of England, while he was a Protestant non conformist.

Scotland had no Test Act and so the young Roebuck came north for the first time to study medicine at the University of Edinburgh. He did well and to complete his medical studies went on to take his degree at what was then the world's leading medical school at the University of Leyden in the Netherlands. It was only when the time came for him to enter practice that he discovered that he did not after all want to follow medicine as a career, because he could not stand the suffering unavoidably inflicted on patients, in those days before the skill of Scottish physicians finally led to the discovery of anaesthetics and antiseptics.

Roebuck therefore decided to turn to his second love, the study of metals and decided to set up his own factory, where he could put his researches to work. Seeking a suitable site, he remembered the lonely stretch of the Forth near Prestonpans where he had often wandered during his student days in Edinburgh. There he set up his first works, which local people soon nicknamed the 'Secret Factory' because of the high walls which Roebuck had built around it and the armed guard he employed to patrol it. The reason for all the security was that he was engaged in experimenting into a new process. Gossip in Prestonpans even had it that the strangely spoken English doctor was dabbling in black magic, because the liquid produced at the 'Secret Factory' was as clear as water but could burn like fire! This was of course sulphuric acid and Roebuck's new lead chamber method of producing it soon enabled him to become the largest producer of the acid in the whole of Britain.

It was while enjoying this success that Roebuck was approached by his neighbour from Cockenzie, Mr William Cadell. Cadell suggested to Roebuck that the time was right for them to become partners in the most ambitious industrial project Scotland had ever seen by exploiting central Scotland's large deposits of ironstone and by building Scotland's first ever large scale foundry to smelt the ore.

1759, Britain's famous year of victories in Canada and India and the year in which Robert Burns was born, saw Roebuck spending the whole of the spring and early summer using his expert knowledge as a metallurgist to discover the richest source of ironstone. This he determined was alongside the coal measures beneath Bo'ness.

When it came to choosing the site for the new ironworks, Roebuck was as careful as he had been over his selection of raw material. To begin with the Cadells considered the new factory should be at a convenient distance from their Cockenzie residence, so that it was out of sight, but within easy travel distance. Roebuck, however, stressed that the choice of location could make or break the new venture. Among the factors to be considered were the nearness of the site to the seams of ironstone; the distance from the ironworks to the Highland forests, because although coal was available alongside the ironstone it was still considered necessary to use wood to make charcoal for the actual smelting; water transport, because the state of Scotland's roads was so bad that it would be necessary both to ship in raw materials and ship out the finished products; finally the site must be on an open stretch of flat ground. Roebuck took advice on all of this from another English industrialist, Samuel Garbett, who had earlier been involved in his sulphuric acid enterprise, and who now along with Cadell became a partner.

At first it seemed the ironworks would be established on the shores of another of the Forth's tributaries, the River Avon near Jinkabout Mill, but in the end the site which became famous at Carron near Falkirk, was chosen. Work began immediately on building the foundry and its furnaces and with a sense of timing, which would be the envy of the modern public relations expert,

Carron Iron Works was officially opened just as dawn broke on New Year's Day 1760. The giant water wheel, bellows and air furnaces, which were all considered among the engineering wonders of their age, had all been started the night before and by first light all was ready for Dr Roebuck to draw off the first molten metal and pour it into a mould in front of the guests, who had been invited to watch the proceedings.

Carron's fame ensured it soon had many distinguished visitors, but some were disappointed by their reception or the lack of it. Robert Burns chanced to arrive on a Sunday in 1787 and true to the Scottish Sabbath, found the works closed and the caretaker refused to admit him. At the time the poet was most annoyed at being turned away. He retreated to the local inn and on one of its window panes vented his spleen by writing the following verses:

> We cam' na here to view your works
> In hopes to be mare wise,
> But only lest we gang to hell,
> It mae be nae surprise;
> But even when we tirled at your door,
> Your Porter thought na hear us;
> Sae may, should we to Hell's yetts come,
> Your Billy Satan sair us.

In the end however he must have forgiven Carron, because when he fitted out Ellisland farmhouse two years later in 1789 he provided his young wife, Jean Armour, with a Carron range, which was considered at the time to be the very latest in kitchen equipment. The famous French writer and historian Foucart was luckier in that he was allowed in, but was furious that he was not allowed to wander as he wished and was prevented from seeing certain sections of the works. This was hardly surprising because much of Carron's success was based on the munitions industry and its innovative short muzzled cannons or Carronades as they became known were soon to play a decisive role in defeating Napoleon both at the Battle of Trafalgar in 1805 and at Waterloo ten years later in 1815. The Carronade was the brain child of the Deputy Governor of the Bank of Scotland, who had also become a director of Carron. Miller was a man of many interests one of which was a great belief in the possibility of harnessing paddle power to propel ships. He is mainly known as the man who put up the money in

1788 to allow William Symington to experiment with the world's first paddle steamer, which led on to the construction of what was perhaps the most famous ship ever built in Grangemouth, the pioneering iron hulled *Charlotte Dundas*. What is less known is that the previous year Miller himself successfully sailed a manually powered paddle boat all the way across the North Sea and through the Baltic to Sweden. The Swedish king was so impressed that he summoned the enterprising Carron director to an audience and presented him with a gold casket. Strangely, inside it was a packet of seeds for a newly discovered root vegetable. Miller brought them home to Scotland, planted them and thus the name swedes.

CHAPTER 9
FROM SEALOCK TO BOOMTOWN

Grangemouth, as its name suggests, stands at the point where the Grange Burn flows into the Forth. Originally, however, it was known as Sealock, because the only reason for its existence was that it was at this somewhat desolate spot on the Stirlingshire shore that Scotland's first canal, the Forth and Clyde, had its eastern terminal.

Until that time Grangemouth or Sealock was just a flat, wind-swept sea marsh and it might well have remained as such had it not been for the drive and ambition of its landowner, Sir Laurence Dundas. For it was Sir Laurence, who realised how much trade the new canal would attract and set about persuading the canal company of the benefits of linking the canal with the Forth at this point on the Forth, rather than further down river at the already well established port of Bo'ness, as was the existing plan. Sir Laurence pointed out that terminating the canal on his estate would save five long miles of digging and that cutting five miles off its length would save an impressive amount of money.

Sir Laurence was successful in his campaign and on 10th June 1768 he was honoured by being invited to dig the first turf to mark the beginning of the canal's thirty five mile course west to Glasgow and the Clyde. It was three years later on a plan dated 1771 that the title The Sealock at the Grange Burn Mouth was first used. Within two years this considerable mouthful was conveniently shortened to Grangemouth.

With the completion of the canal in 1790, as Dundas had predicted Grangemouth's trade boomed as it now provided east coast access to Glasgow, which was at that time the country's fastest developing city.

The new port of Grangemouth soon applied for and was successful in gaining its own customs house, which was es-tablished in a fine grey stone building in North Harbour Street. This robbed Bo'ness of all the customs dues, which it had until then been levying on all goods imported and exported through Grangemouth, in exactly the same way that it had in its turn earlier deprived Blackness of its revenues a century before.

Grangemouth also enjoyed the great advantage over Bo'ness that it was situated on flat ground, whereas its rival was hemmed in by steep hills. Thus when in the 1840s the coming of the railways replaced the canal as the most convenient method of inland transport, Grangemouth again had an advantage over Bo'ness. While railway lines fanned out throughout the whole area of Grangemouth docks, Bo'ness had to make do with the single track Slammanan Railway, which linked it with the main Glasgow to Edinburgh line at Mannual Junction near Polmont.

The rivalry between Grangemouth and Bo'ness and to almost the same extent with its even nearer neighbour Falkirk, did much to help create a community spirit amongst 'Portonians' as its inhabitants became proud to call themselves. This pride was increased still further by the model town, which the Dundas family created for them to live in. With the exception of Edinburgh's Georgian New Town, Grangemouth was the first planned town in Scotland and later it also became Scotland's first miniature garden city.

Sir Laurence's idea was to design his new town in the shape of a ship, with broad main streets running from stem to stern. He died in 1781 before his scheme was accomplished, but the town which was built between then and 1800 under his son's supervision did keep to many of the high standards which he had laid down. These included broad streets, forty feet wide with all house fronts strictly in line, just as he had admired in James Craig's design for the New Town in Edinburgh. Although Grangemouth's new houses were planned for the seaport's dockers and their families and not the capital's rich upper classes, they were nonetheless very well built and well finished with many scrolls, mouldings and other decorative touches to their stone exteriors.

During the 19th century the Dundas family kept up to date with the latest ideas in town planning and in 1861 decided the time was right to expand Grangemouth still further into a miniature garden city. The New Town as it became known, in contrast to the original Old Town, which had grown up around the canal basin, spread east out towards the Grange Burn. Every house in the new development was surrounded by an attractive garden.

By the time Grangemouth's first Town Councillors or Commissioners, as they were at first called, took over from the Dundas

The hustle and bustle of Grangemouth's old town is well captured in this late 19th-century print. The old town clock and the Queen's Hotel beyond it in South Bridge Street can be seen.

family on 30th December 1872, Grangemouth was considered as fine as any new town in Scotland and on that same date by the Lindsay Act of Parliament it became a burgh.

The Commissioners were all prominent local businessmen such as timber mill owners Daniel Alexander McLaren and Hugh McPherson and they maintained the same high standards set by the Dundas family, when they came to pass plans for the ever expanding garden city. Its main thoroughfare was Bo'ness Road which ran over the bridge across the Grange Burn and on out all the way east to the bridge over the River Avon. It was on Bo'ness Road that Commissioners McLaren and McPherson built the finest of homes for themselves and their families. Mr McPherson developed Inch House, which had until then been a farm out in the countryside, while Mr McLaren built the stone turreted Avondhu. While the former was demolished in the 1960s to make way for a hideous modern petrol filling station, the latter still stands, but sadly it has been robbed of its once beautiful tree lined garden, which has been cleared for a housing development.

At the docks too, there was steady progress throughout these years. By 1838 it was clear that the basin at the entrance to the

Forth and Clyde Canal could not cope with all the trade it had created and that a proper dock was required. Consultant engineers were commissioned and their report resulted in the building of what has become known as the Old Dock. It was opened in 1843 and the first vessels sailed in through the dock gates which gave access from the River Carron. It was soon clear even more dock space was needed and this was created by enlarging the Junction Canal between the Old Dock and the timber basin and the new Junction dock came into use in 1859.

In 1867 Grangemouth received a tremendous boost when the docks were acquired by the Caledonian Railway Company, which also purchased the Forth and Clyde Canal. Between 1867 and 1875 the tonnage handled at Grangemouth almost doubled and the railway company eager for further expansion decided to dredge the muddy Carron to enable larger vessels to sail into the port and to build a big new dock to accommodate them. It was aimed to dredge the Carron to a depth of eight metres, but despite round the clock dredging this was never achieved because as fast as the mud was scooped up by the early bucket dredgers, the silt piled up again. Despite this set-back when the new Carron Dock with its wider dock gates leading from the river was officially opened in 1882, it proved very successful. By 1896 cargo tonnage handled at Grangemouth reached almost two and a half million tons.

The dredging problem on the Carron proved insuperable and so in 1897 the railway company decided the only solution was to build new lock gates linking the port directly with the Forth for the first time. At the same time parliamentary approval was obtained for a huge expansion of the whole port by creating a new dock covering thirty acres, a smaller basin covering ten acres and deep water channels to connect them both to the new dock gates and to the other existing docks. In addition a new twenty three acre timber basin to allow more imported wood to be seasoned was planned, making a total of almost one hundred additional acres of water in the port area. Contracts were issued in 1898 and the whole new complex of docks, basins and channels came into service in 1906. The excellent new facilities proved so successful that within three years Grangemouth's imports and exports reached almost four million tons.

Grangemouth's success was dealt a devastating blow, when at the outbreak of the First World War, the Admiralty closed it to all

Grange Street ran at right angles to South Bridge Street in Grangemouth's old town, which was one of the first planned town centres in the country.

merchant shipping. During the four years of the hostilities against Germany a few cargo vessels did regularly enter and leave the port. They looked just like the usual 'dirty British coasters with their salt caked smoke stacks', which John Masefield celebrated in his famous poem, but they were not as innocent as they appeared. For these were the famous 'Q' ships, whose superstructures were carefully altered to conceal powerful hidden guns. Under the direction of Commander Gordon Campbell these apparently vulnerable unarmed merchantmen deliberately set out to lure enemy naval vessels into attacking them, then as soon as they were within range, the red duster was struck, the Royal Navy's white ensign hoisted and their guns went pounding into action. Commander Campbell and his crews were responsible for sinking seven U-boats and he was awarded the VC.

The signing of the armistice in November 1918 was followed by a post war trade boom and in 1923 Grangemouth's imports and exports rose to over four million tons, a record breaking figure not exceeded for a further forty years. 1923 was also a very significant year for Grangemouth as a port for two other reasons. Firstly its owner the Caledonian Railway Company was taken over by the London, Midland and Scottish Railway, the famous LMS, which at the time was the largest joint-stock company in the world and

71

which ensured more than adequate financial backing for the dock. Secondly Scottish Oils chose Grangemouth as the site for its new oil refinery, a move which was to have enormous consequences for not just the port but the whole town and its surrounding area.

Until that time Scottish Oils had solely processed oil from the rich deposits of shale, which the industry's founder, Dr James 'Paraffin' Young, had discovered in West and Midlothian back in the 1860s and its operations had centred around the Calders villages and Broxburn, with its headquarters at Middleton Hall in Uphall. Now in the booming 1920s it proved itself very forward looking by realising that it must become involved in the development of the overseas oil industry in the Gulf or rather the Persian Gulf, as it was at that time always described. Grangemouth was chosen as the ideal place where the imported crude oil could be processed, yet still close enough to the Scottish shale oil fuel for the refinery to manufacture its products, should the foreign venture prove less successful than anticipated. The growth in the imported oil business was, however, satisfactorily swift and the first deepwater oil jetties in Grangemouth's Eastern Channel were commissioned in 1924. This was followed by a second major development of tanker berths in 1931. Two years later a new record was established for the largest cargo ever handled at Grangemouth, when the tanker *Athel Princess* discharged 13,446 tonnes of crude oil from Abadan. This sounds small compared to the huge loads of refined oil exported daily down river at British Petroleum's Hound Island Complex off the shore at Dalmeny to the east of the Forth Bridge, but in the 1930s this import was headline news and no-one could even have imagined the change in the oil market and the exports, which were to follow half a century later!

Grangemouth hit the national headlines again at the end of the 1930s as one of the country's prime development areas, when it was announced at the beginning of February 1939 that the newly formed Scottish Aviation Ltd had chosen it as the site for a new airport to serve both Edinburgh and Glasgow. Not only that, the new company proudly declared in *The Scotsman* that the first passenger flights from Grangemouth's new aerodrome would take off in only three months time!

This tremendous rush of enthusiasm was created by the publication of the Maybury Report. It stated that, 'as the country

surrounding both Edinburgh and Glasgow cannot provide individual airports to the required standard in close proximity, Scotland
should have one central airport, situated between the two cities.'

With the backing of aviation enthusiast Lord Nigel Douglas
Hamilton, who was himself an amateur pilot, plus the expertise of
Squadron Leader D F McIntyre from Prestwick, Scottish Aviation
Ltd under the chairmanship of London based Mr W E Nixon and
with Mr R L Angus and Mr T P Mills as its other directors, was
quickly established. These enterprising businessmen went out and
drove around central Scotland searching for their ideal site and
finally announced they had found it on the shores of the Forth to
the south east of Grangemouth. Surprisingly the fact Scottish Oils
Ltd already had its expanding oil refinery immediately between
the chosen site and the river did not appear to deter the directors
of Scottish Aviation, because in the prospectus for their imaginative
new venture they stated, 'This piece of land is one of the few in
the country where the natural contours assist flying and where
man-made obstructions do not exist'.

With an optimism, which today would seem not only naive but
quite absurd, they went on to announce that, 'One of the most
remarkable features of the establishment of this massive airport is
the fact that contractors have guaranteed to complete the job
within three months. Work will commence on Monday 6th
February and the aerodrome will be opened on 1st May'. This
Scottish Aviation boasted, 'was the dawning of a new age for flying
in Scotland'.

Over the next weekend deals were finalised between the
owners of six adjacent farms, Abbotsgrange, Bowhouse, Claret,
Dalgleish's Reddock, Roy's Redock and Wholeflats and by Sunday
evening Scottish Aviation owned the five hundred and fifty acres
they needed for work to begin. And begin it did the very next
morning, when as dawn broke on that cold damp February
Monday, the contractor's vehicles rolled onto the site. By nine
o'clock there was a near riot at Grangemouth's labour exchange
as crowds of men, many unemployed throughout the whole
depression of the 1930s, clamoured to be hired for the new
development. The police had to be called and the doors closed
until more staff could be drafted in to deal with all the new recruits.

Amazingly the contractors kept their word and within the space
of twelve weeks the imposing light grey coloured control tower,

The houses of Canal Street were reflected in the still waters of the Forth and Clyde Canal, while a boy played on a raft of timber just in front of the lock gates.

passenger terminal buildings and large aircraft hangars were all completed and handed over on Thursday 29th April 1939. The only change from the original prospectus was the name of the airport. Instead of calling it Edinburgh Airport as at first intended it was decided it would be more appropriate to call it Scottish Central Airport. Whether this was to avoid petty jealousy with Glasgow, or whether it was simply a more accurate geographical description was not explained, but instead of changing the first part of the title it would actually have been more appropriate to have changed the second part from airport to airfield.

For while the new Scottish Central Airport did indeed have splendid terminal buildings in the very latest streamlined architectural style of the 1930s, it did not have one single tarmac runway, because even the largest passenger planes of the period could still take off and land on a grass strip and Grangemouth was very proud to announce that it had the longest grass runway in Scotland, 800 yards wide and 1,100 yards long, double the size of the one at Renfrew, which had been the previous largest and that by June it would be extended to 1,300 yards wide and 1,500 yards in length, making it the largest in the whole of the United Kingdom.

Within days of the handover by the contractors the new Central Scotland Airport was officially opened by Air-Marshall Viscount

Tall cranes tower over the bows of a large vessel taking shape on the slipway of the Grangemouth Dockyard Company's yard on the shores of the River Carron. On the landward side of the yard, the Company's unusual block of offices is reflected in the placid waters of the Forth and Clyde Canal, with the houses of Canal Street stretching into the background. The most famous ship ever built at Grangemouth was the world's first successful steamship, which sailed on the canal and is represented in the town's coat of arms. The size of ships built at Grangemouth was always limited by the fact that they had to be launched sideways into the narrow Carron.

Trenchard on the afternoon of Saturday 1st May. To mark the occasion his lordship started the propeller of a miniature aeroplane set on a silver cigar box, which was later presented to him. The starting of the little aeroplane's engine triggered a smoke bomb on the newly laid turf in front of the airport terminal building's passenger lounge, through whose large plate glass windows the invited guests had a grandstand view of the whole ceremony. As the smoke cleared they saw a whole flight of nine Hawker-Hart aircraft flying in formation round the perimeter of the new aerodrome, which was circular in shape. As the excited crowd watched, each of the Hawker-Harts touched down and taxied to a halt in front of the three storey high control tower on whose facade was embossed Scottish Aviation Ltd's proud symbol of a winged lion's head. Highlight of the day was the arrival of Grangemouth's first international flight flown by one of the largest planes ever seen in Scotland up until that date, a McDonald Douglas C3 belonging to Royal Dutch Airlines, KLM. As the KLM officials descended the steps from their plane they informed the waiting reporters and photographers that they intended to launch a service from Grangemouth to Amsterdam with a flight time of only two and a half hours, thus updating all of the Forth Valley's long standing links with their country.

The honour of starting Grangemouth's first time tabled passenger flights, went however, to North Eastern Airways, whose first planes took off on the following Monday morning and whose 1939 summer timetable boasted that flights had been carefully timed to coincide with the arrival of trains form Glasgow and Edinburgh at nearby Polmont Station from which a specially chartered motor coach would convey intending passengers direct to the aerodrome.

More ominous was the fact that on that same May Monday morning Flight Lieutenant I E C Watson also arrived at the aerodrome to take charge of training Royal Airforce volunteer reservists. For the storm clouds of war were gathering and Grangemouth's first successful summer season of passenger flights was also to be its last. On Sunday 3rd September the British government declared war on Germany and at the same time all civilian flights were suspended indefinitely. The aerodrome was taken over by the Air Ministry and from then on the aerodrome became an RAF base. Two tarmac runways were laid, the main one stretching east almost to the shore of the River Avon and pilot training began. The young pilots came not only from all over Britain but from all of the Commonwealth airforces as well as Poland. Under the direction of Commanding Officer, Group Captain D V Carnegie, Blenheims, Gladiators, Lysanders, Spitfires and Whirlwinds and the short-lived Defiants filled the air above Grangemouth and the surrounding Stirlingshire countryside. Not all of them returned safely and the girls of Paton and Baldwins knitwear factory on the shores of the river midway between Grangemouth and Bo'ness wept as the pilot of the plane who had just seconds earlier dipped his wings to them as they enjoyed their lunchtime break, died as his engine cut out and he spiralled down to his death in the dark waters of the Forth. On a lighter note among the many support crew was a young English national serviceman, who was really more interested in becoming a comedian. He gave one of his first performances at Grangemouth Town Hall, where the programme gave Max Bygraves one of his

A snowy day on the banks of the Grange Burn, the tributary which joins the Forth at Grangemouth and from which the town takes its name.

earliest billings. After the end of the Second World War in 1945, Grangemouth was retained as an RAF training station and its Tiger Moth bi-planes and gliders, became familiar sights as they practised take-offs and landings. By the time the RAF departed, Edinburgh's Turnhouse and Glasgow's Renfrew airports were well established and Grangemouth never regained the commercial and passenger traffic which had seemed to offer such promise in the heady spring days of 1939. Once during the 1960s it was proposed to re-establish a Central Scotland Airport. While the spread of the oil refinery obviously made it impossible to consider the site of the original aerodrome, the flat farm land around Skinflats was surveyed, but in the end it was decided to build Glasgow Airport to the west of the city at Abbotsinch with all the resultant ground transportation problems and to upgrade Turnhouse into Edinburgh Airport. Thus the opportunity to create one central super airport for the whole of Scotland was lost forever and the realisation of what Grangemouth might have become had it not been for the outbreak of hostilities in 1939 remained only a dream.

The Second World War was also a disaster for Grangemouth Docks. Trade fell from two and a half million tons in 1939 to only one and a half million tons in 1940 and although the port remained open the danger to oil tankers sailing in and out of the Forth, forced the closure of the refinery through lack of supplies.

Once peace came, however, Grangemouth's rise was meteoric with two massive expansion schemes at the by then British Petroleum Refinery leading to it being nicknamed 'Scotland's boom town', with the country's fastest expanding population. Much of the new refinery, complete with its own electricity generating station with its distinctive tall towers and the equally impressive steam capped cooling towers, was built on land reclaimed from the Forth and many of the buildings were provided with special raft like foundations. Other oil related industries were established along the length of Bo'ness Road, while on the other side of the town at Earls Gates, in the grounds of the Earl of Zetland's Dundas Family's former home, Kerse House, ICI or the 'chemical works' as they were always known doubled in size. As well as Paints Division, where the first true green paint was discovered in pre-war days, ICI now expanded across Falkirk Road, where a new pharma-ceutical plant was established. Both sites are now operated by ICI off-shoot Zeneca and the eastern part of the grounds has been turned into Project Jupiter Wildlife Garden, which welcomes visitors to see this unusual example of urban conservation. A novel feature is the fact that the bird hide doubles as an emergency shelter just in case of an explosion at the nearby plant, but thankfully it has never needed to be used.

While Project Jupiter is growing many species of native Scottish trees, the area surrounding it has always been famous as the site of Grangemouth's imported timber yards. Several still flourish, but sadly not the best known, Muirheads, which was equally famous for its world champion pipe band and its development of prelaminated timber, including the material for the construction of the controversial crown of thorns on top of Linlithgow's St Michael's Kirk.

All of this trade meant a consistent growth in trade at the docks. In 1948, as a result of the nationalisation of the railways, the port came under the control of the British Transport Commission and it was under their auspices that, in 1959, a major development scheme for the port was instigated. This comprised the flush surfacing of all the quays, the recranage of the Grange Dock, the construction of three new transit sheds and the modernisation of the existing sheds.

The port remained under the control of the British Transport

Commission for fifteen years but in 1963 the British Transport Docks Board assumed responsibility for all nationalised ports. Their policy was one of continued expansion and led to the construction of new roadways, additional shed accommodation and a Common User Oil Jetty which was commissioned in 1966. About this time a new larger and deeper entrance lock was being planned, but for a number of reasons these plans did not come to fruition.

One of the most important events in the port's history occurred during the period of the Docks Board's control, this being the inauguration, in April 1966, of the first fully containerised deep-sea liner service from any United Kingdom port. The service was introduced by Sea-Land Inc and operated between Rotterdam, Bremen, Grangemouth and New York. The first vessels were equipped with their own container handling equipment, but in 1967 two container transporter cranes were commissioned.

In January 1969 the Forth Ports Authority was formed under an Act of Parliament and Grangemouth then became part of an esturial Port Authority comprising of six ports; Leith, Granton, Methil, Burntisland and Kirkcaldy. However, expansion and im-provements continued, the most important being the construction of the New Entrance Lock, work on which commenced in 1970. This lock was opened on 26th September 1974 and has a length of 237 metres, width 29.1 metres and depth at high tide of 11.7 metres. The opening of the New Entrance Lock has permitted the entry to the Port of much larger tankers (up to 25,000 cwt) and the increased dimensions make the passage of large vessels much simpler and speedier.

Further developments at Grangemouth were mainly connected with the expansion of BP's jetty facilities. The old Entrance Lock was converted into a specialist LPG berth. The area on the North side of the Eastern Channel was leased to BP.

Over the years the sound of the docks has changed entirely from the clanging of shunting railway wagons and the shrill whistles of impatient steam engines to the revving of lorry engines and the warning bleepers of reversing fork lift trucks. For Grangemouth's trade has become mainly containerised and under its enterprising new owners Forth Ports Plc, this aspect of its business has become so successful that it is now the busiest dock in the whole of Scotland. Two massive blue container cranes on

The full extent of Grangemouth docks can be appreciated from this aerial view, looking south from the modern dock entrance. Notice the steaming cooling towers of the British Petroleum oil refinery on the left, and in the centre the tank farm at the Common User Jetty, with, to the right, the muddy river Carron snaking its slow way inward towards Grangemouth Dockyard Company's shipbuilding yard. Forth Ports Plc.

the South Quay handle sixty thousand 'boxes' as the dockers call them and container ships sail in and out daily round the clock, instead of having to wait for high tides as vessels had to in past decades. Five highly trained teams of operators now ensure the dock gates can be opened at any time of the day or night and times past when the 'Leakies', the unusual tides which gave Grangemouth the advantage of high water twice over every twelve hours, are now forgotten. Five times a week container ships with their decks piled high with these huge metal boxes, sail in and out from Rotterdam where many of the containers are transhipped to even larger vessels to be transported on across the Atlantic and world wide. Three times a week whole loads of containers are shipped in and out from Antwerp, twice a week from the River Thames and once a week from Hamburg, this German service also providing a roll-on roll-off ferry service for commercial vehicles. These trucks can be loaded and unloaded at any time because of

This second aerial view of Grangemouth Docks looks in the opposite direction north across the Forth to the tall chimney of Longannet Power Station on the Fife shore. It is actually four smokestacks wrapped in one, and the largest chimney of its type in Europe. Forth Ports Plc.

the constant level of water maintained twenty four hours a day throughout the port. In addition Grangemouth has a specially strengthened 'ro-ro' berth at which exceptionally heavy loads in excess of 600 tons, such as special equipment for the oil refinery, can roll directly on and off the ships on which they have been transported. The trouble comes when these exceptional loads have to proceed ashore and in the past Grangemouth's street lights and telephone wires have had to be removed to allow their progress through the town.

Despite all of this activity and record breaking cargo totals exceeding eight million tons a year, Grangemouth's labour force has been drastically reduced from the thousands of dockers who used to clock on each day to a total of only seventy one highly skilled port operators. The job demarcation disputes of old are long gone and Grangemouth's stevedores are now well-known for their multi-skilled approach, which ensures ships are turned round in hours rather than the days and even weeks that they once remained in port. To speed up trade even further Grangemouth is linked by computer to the National Maritime Cargo Processing System, which gives firms the benefit of computerised customs clearance of their cargoes.

One cargo which has remained important throughout all of Grangemouth's two hundred years history is timber. This import trade has now been expanded and the modern purpose built Forest Products Terminal on the North Quay now also handles wood pulp, paper and a wide range of board products. One of the most dramatic cargoes to see handled at Grangemouth are the enormous rolls of newsprint on which future editions of all the Scottish national papers are printed. Looking like toilet rolls for giants, they require extra specially careful handling as an inch deep gash can render thousands of metres of paper unusable. Sixteen thousand metres of transit shed accommodation is available at the Forest Product Terminal as well as a wide area of open quayside for those customers who prefer to unload their paper straight onto waiting trucks and trailers. In all over 200,000 tons of forest products are handled each year.

Perhaps the part of the port which seems to have changed least over the years is the East Quay, where a wide range of bulk cargoes including clay, coal, slag, sand, soda ash, salt, vermiculite and bauxite to make aluminium are all unloaded by four ten ton grabbing cranes and two fifty ton controlled discharge hoppers. In all over 200,000 tons of this type of cargo are landed every year and two fifty ton weighbridges are situated within the docks to make sure there is a minimum of delay in moving these loads on to the Scottish factories which require them as their raw materials.

Other cargoes regularly shipped through Grangemouth range from shining sheet steel to sticky molasses, the latter stored in tanks over beside the petrol tanks at what is known as the Common User Jetty. The thought of what might happen if the pipes ever became crossed is mind boggling!

The Common User Jetty is a most interesting part of the docks as it is from here all day long that fleets of road tankers ferry petrol to filling stations all over Scotland and the North of England and this berth takes its name from the fact that different companies simply hire tank storage space as and when they require it. Ross Chemicals who own the storage tank complex are well used to handling a wide range of chemicals and fuels and has established an excellent safety record for dealing with what can be dangerous cargoes. While most of the crude processed at the Grangemouth oil refinery is now piped direct from the North Sea Oil Field, British Petroleum still has several of its own berths on the north side of the dock complex and piped cargoes still make up a considerable proportion of the port's trade.

One trade which many local people have long wished that Grangemouth would develop is a direct passenger car ferry service to Scandinavia, but with already well established routes from the north of England to Norway, Denmark, Belgium and the Netherlands, the establishment of a Scottish route would be a difficult challenge. Apart from the overnight passenger service to London operated by the Carron Company ships in Victorian times, Grangemouth has never been a passenger port, with the exception of the 1960s visits of the famous school ship *Dunera*, which MP for Linlithgow, Tam Dalyell, helped to launch and occasional calls during the 1980s by the two floating Bible book shop ships, *Doulos* and *Logos*. Most recent passenger vessel to call at Grangemouth was the world's last sea-going paddle steamer *Waverley*, whose down river cruises recalled the pre-war pleasure trips of the 1920s and 1930s operated by Wilson's Tugs, Galloway's Steamers and in particular by the famous *Fair Maid*. The *Fair Maid* was as much loved on the Forth as any of the Clyde steamers on the west coast and many older members of the community still recall with fond affection Sunday School outings on summer Saturdays to the Silver Sands at Aberdour, the shows at Burntisland and the cliffs at Kinghorn. On long light summer nights the *Fair Maid* also operated popular evening dance cruises with a live band playing on deck to provide the music, a tradition which the modern pleasure vessel *Maid of the Forth* has happily recently revived with her regular weekend jazz cruises and occasional Three Bridges ceilidh cruises from Queensferry's Hawes Pier.

These latter voyages take the 'Maid' sailing past Grangemouth as she voyages up river to Kincardine Bridge, but while she has brought pleasure cruising back to the Forth, there is sadly not a glimpse to be caught of the town's now long forgotten seaside. This was the famous Shelly Bank at the mouth of the Grange Burn, but this once very popular strand of shingle, where many Portonian families spent happy holiday days in the 1920s, has long since disappeared.

Today any holiday references to Grangemouth are generally facetious comparisons with Blackpool's famous illuminations as the thousands of lights and many flares of the oil refinery brighten the night sky for over twenty miles around with their orange glow. It is perhaps by dark that the spread of the huge refinery is best appreciated as it sprawls across the River Avon, and over the low-lying Carse of Kinneil all the way to the outskirts of Bo'ness. The sluggishly slow flowing Avon formerly marked the boundary between Stirlingshire and West Lothian and until twenty years ago, the little stone built toll house, where all traffic had formerly to stop and pay, still stood on the Grangemouth side of the bridge over the river. Now Falkirk Unitary Authority, which superseded Falkirk District on 1st April 1996, controls the river front all the way down stream through Bo'ness to Blackness.

Once over the Avon Bridge the road makes a sharp left-hand turn at the recently built roundabout and skirts the edge of Kinneil Woods as it passes the Water Ins, a place name which recalls how far the river used to come up and how much land has since been reclaimed from the Forth. On the river side of the road stand the buildings originally occupied by Paton and Baldwins knitwear factory. They are now the headquarters for one of Britain's best known packaging firms, whose business includes regular ship-ments of goods ranging from school uniforms to Christmas presents to the people of the Falkland Islands for whom it acts as a kind of distant general store.

Quarter of a mile further on modern road developments now bypass the former bottle neck at the narrow low Crawyett, the Crow's Gate as the old stone bridge carrying the Bo'ness to Polmont railway line, is still known. Now the road beneath the bridge leads solely to Kinneil Estate and the steep brae ahead was the start of the famous hillclimb, which provided so many thrills and sometimes spills during 1950s and 1960s summer weekends as Ninian Sanderson in his saltire-blue Jaguar of Ecurie Ecosse and many other famous racing drivers of the period, vied to knock seconds off the fastest times with Raymond Baxter providing the commentary for radio listeners as the cars hurtled up the hill, through the Courtyard and Snake Bends. Sadly new housing developments of the 1970s put a stop to this exciting form of motor sport. Now Kinneil is a much quieter place, but one still worth the detour to explore.

CHAPTER 10
DRAMATIC KINNEIL

After the pancake flat surroundings of Grangemouth, Kinneil stands dramatically on the edge of the ancient raised beach, four miles further down river. This striking setting, high on its hill overlooking the Forth, seems strangely appropriate because Kinneil has down through the centuries been the scene of many diverse dramas.

The name Kinneil means Wall's End and it was thought for many years that Antonine's Wall, the farthest flung outermost defence of the Roman Empire had its eastern terminus at this spot on the Forth, until in Victorian times local geologist Henry M Cadell of the House of Grange, who has already been mentioned in connection with the Moss Lairds, proved through his excavations that the fortification actually stretched to the other side of Bo'ness to end on the shore at Bridgeness.

Kinneil is however still an excellent site to study the Roman occupation of this part of Scotland by visiting the foundations of one of the fortlets, which occurred at intervals along the whole length of the thirty five mile long wall and which has now been excavated.

The wall was erected around 140 AD during the governorship of Lollius Urbicus and in the reign of Emperor Antoninus in whose honour it was named. Unlike the stone-built Hadrian's Wall on the borders of Scotland and England to the south, this most northerly line of defence consisted mainly of a rampart of earth and sods of turf. It varied in height between three and four metres and in front was a vallum or ditch over thirteen metres wide and over six metres deep to provide extra security and act as an additional deterrent.

To be sent to man the long cold windswept reaches of Antonine's Wall on its route across Scotland from Bo'ness on the Forth to Castlehill near Old Kilpatrick on the Clyde, was looked upon as very much a punishment posting by the Romans and the wall was garrisoned mainly by auxiliaries from Gaul and other conquered lands. Some of these foreign auxiliaries stayed in

Scotland for many years and excavations along the stretch of Antonine's Wall from Bridgeness to Kinneil have produced evidence, including an elaborately carved stone altar, that intermarriage with local women took place.

The Roman altar and the other Bo'ness finds are now on display in the National Museum of Scotland in Edinburgh's Queen Street, leaving only a replica of the Latin inscription on the site at Bridgeness. One of the Bo'ness carvings on show in the museum depicts Roman cavalry trampling the native Picts under foot, but in the end the relentlessly repeated attacks persuaded the Romans that Antonine's Wall was not really worth the cost of defending and at the beginning of the fourth century they withdrew.

Tradition has it that the successful local leader at the time was called Grime and it is said that it was from his name that a local section of the wall became known as Grahamsdyke, a title it still bears to this day. Far from being a hero, however, Grime appears to have been regarded as a villain because the early predecessors of Bo'ness mothers living on what they considered the more civilised southern side of the wall are said to have threatened badly behaved children that he would come and carry them off in true bogeyman fashion!

After the departure of the Romans and their troops, the next mention of Kinneil does not occur until nine centuries later, but again it is in connection with warfare and indeed Scotland's most famous battle. For it was as a reward for services rendered to King Robert the Bruce as part of his royal bodyguard at Bannockburn that the Barony of Kinneil was granted to Sir Gilbert Hamilton. The King's choice of Kinneil as a prize for Hamilton was particularly appropriate because it was on Kinneil Muir that he performed his greatest service for the Scottish monarch as it was there he slew the Great Lieutenant of England. Who the Great Lieutenant was has never been discovered, but it is possible that a huge stone, which used to stand close to the Linlithgow to Falkirk road to the west of Linlithgow Bridge, may have marked his grave.

At the same time that he granted Kinneil to Gilbert Hamilton, King Robert the Bruce also bestowed on him a coat of arms consisting of, 'three sink fuilzies in ane bludy field' or 'three cinquefois on a scarlet ground' as it was later translated in heraldic terms, to mark his, 'true service and great manhood'. Sir Gilbert's importance in Scottish affairs was clearly recognised later when he had the opportunity to return the compliments when he gave the funeral oration at the burial of the Bruce's body in Dunfermline Abbey.

It is perhaps only fair to report that there is a less romantic version of how Kinneil came into the possession of the Hamilton family. This claims King Robert granted the estate to Gilbert's son Walter in 1323 despite the fact that Walter had actually fought on the side of the English at Bannockburn and had only changed sides after the Bruce's soldiers captured Bothwell Castle of which he was in charge of defending! Having seen the patriotic light, however, young Walter was clearly forgiven by his monarch because shortly afterwards he was knighted by King Robert.

No matter how the Hamiltons came to own Kinneil, it is definite that they soon built a tall thick stone walled peel tower high above the rocky ravine of the Gil Burn at the point where it crashes down the hillside to the Forth. This was an excellent defensive site and parts of the original keep with its narrow arrow-slit windows and gun ports still towers above the burn. By the late 16th century more peaceful times came to Scotland and the Hamiltons felt they could safely live more comfortably in the typically Scottish 'L' shaped mansion, which they added to the site to the north east of the peel.

The following century, one of the most interesting members of the Hamilton family, the Duchess Anna, who gained Bo'ness its burgh status in 1668, added still further impressive additions to Kinneil House, linking the mansion to the old peel tower with a balustrated central block crowned with a roof top cupola. Soon her fine home became known as the Palace of Kinneil.

Following the execution of King Charles I in 1649 one of the Roundhead officers ordered north by the new Lord High Protector Oliver Cromwell to police Scotland was one General Lilbourne, who made his headquarters at Kinneil. Having married only a short time before his posting, General Lilbourne realising his stay in Scotland might be a long one, decided to bring his young and very beautiful wife, the Lady Alice, with him to take up residence at Kinneil. Unfortunately Lord and Lady Lilbourne's marriage was not a happy one. Lady Alice was very homesick and there were frequent rows and quarrels. In the end the General decided to teach his disobedient wife a lesson by ordering her to be locked up in a small attic room at the top of the west side of the keep.

Lady Lilbourne was not, however, to be so easily quelled and late one night succeeded in escaping from her turret prison. Silently she made her way down the steep stone spiral stairs and succeeded in slipping out of the house. Then, clad only in her diaphanous billowing white nightgown, she fled down the pitch-dark tree lined drive towards the lights of the miners' homes at Castleloan. Just as she was almost within reach of the houses, she heard her husband and his servants and their dogs giving chase. Desperately she sought a hiding place. The sound of her pursuers and the baying of the hounds was growing ever closer. It was too far to reach the cottages. Just as they were almost upon her she spotted a hollow tree. Swiftly she climbed into the bough and sighed with relief as her husband and his entourage thundered past. Down below her, she heard the search party wakening all the miners' families and searching their small homes, but all, of course, to no avail. Angrily and noisily her husband and his searchers made their way back towards Kinneil. All might have been well had it not been for a wisp of her white nightgown. As he past the hollow tree, Lord Lilbourne chanced to look up and saw the tiny patch of white material. In seconds Lady Lilbourne was recaptured and with the dogs rending the dark of the night with their savage barks, was hauled back to the big house.

Even after this experience Lady Alice refused to submit to her husband. Once again she was imprisoned in the room high in the keep. This time Lady Lilbourne chose the only other way to escape that she knew was certain. She flung herself out of the narrow window and plunged down and down and down to die almost two hundred feet below on the rock-strewn bed of the Gil Burn.

Lady Lilbourne's tragic suicide did not however end her sad connection with Kinneil, because ever since the 'White Lady' as she became known because of the give-away white nightgown, has haunted the old house, her shrieks, screams and wails echoing eerily through its now ruined halls and corridors on dark winter nights. By day too, over three hundred years after her death, Lady Lilbourne is still remembered as local children visiting Kinneil Estate seldom miss a chance to chant the old local rhyme, 'Poor Lady Lilbourne died in the Gil Burn'.

While local families still enjoy picnicking in the picturesque grounds of Kinneil, it is disappointing that they are no longer able to explore the house. It is supposed to be looked after by Historic

One of the earliest Bo'ness fair days, it is thought to be the second fair, and this may be the only existing record of a fair day at Kinneil House. John Doherty.

Scotland, but that body has not seen fit to open it to the public for several years. This is a great pity because Kinneil has many interesting features, especially the fine wall murals of religious scenes. It was these Italian masterpieces, including ones showing the story of the Good Samaritan, which saved Kinneil, when its previous guardian Bo'ness Town Council, decided to demolish it in the 1930s. Fortunately the workmen noticed the huge wall pictures, which had been hidden beneath layers of plaster and stopped the demolition.

Even denied access to the house, Kinneil has much to offer in its beautiful grounds. Even older than the Roman remains in the field to the south west are the impressive fossilised remains of tree trunks, which are situated behind the house. Opposite them is a small ruined building. This was where the famous Scottish inventor, Greenock born James Watt came to work in secret on his improvements to the steam engine, which was eventually to revolutionise British industry.

Watt was persuaded to come to Kinneil by Dr John Roebuck, of Carron Iron Works fame, who had rented the big house from the Duke of Hamilton as a suitable home for his family, at the same time that he came to Bo'ness to oversee the working of the local pits, where he acquired the mineral rights to ensure a supply of ironstone and coal for Carron. The main problem he discovered with the pits at Kinneil was that production was frequently interrupted by the underground workings being flooded by in-rushes of water from the Forth. From the Cornish tin mines he had one of Newcomen's new fangled steam engines brought north to Kinneil to pump out the flood water, but it could not cope with the inrushes of river water. It was then that Roebuck heard of the innovations being made by James Watt, who was carrying out research at the University of Glasgow.

At first Watt wrote to Roebuck stating that his health would not permit him to undertake the arduous thirty mile ride from the city to Kinneil, but in the end his lack of money to continue his experiments and Roebuck's offer of funds, persuaded him to change his mind. At last Watt arrived mounted on horse back and to the excitement of the Roebuck children, clutching a working model of his improved steam engine. After Watt had rested in one of the bedrooms overlooking the river and been entertained to refreshments and dinner, the big dining room table was cleared and Watt set up the little miniature engine. Watched by the six young Roebucks, who had been allowed to stay up for the meal, because of their distinguished visitor he demonstrated his idea for conserving energy and making the engine much more efficient by providing it with a separate condensing cylinder.

Dr Roebuck was convinced Watt was on to the right idea and next morning had the inventor installed in the little rectangular stone workshop above the Gil Burn. This secluded hide-away provided Watt with the security to conduct his experiments with the secrecy which nowadays would be accorded developments in nuclear research. Visiting the workshop in 1965, Dr Roebuck's descendant, Senator The Hon Arthur W Roebuck QC, Attorney General for Ontario, recounted a family tradition. According to it the doctor was present in the workshop one day when he noticed that as pressure developed in the newly designed engine, steam escaped around the piston, where it came through the cylinder head. Quickly Roebuck whipped off one of his leather top boots, cut off a round, wrapped it round the piston and thus made the first steam packing.

The Roebuck children also used to make their way down to the workshop as often as they were allowed and Watt often took time off from his experiments on the steam engine to make them toys, including a small working mandolin, which he gave to Elizabeth, the only girl.

Unfortunately this little stringed instrument appears to have worked better then the first of the new steam engines, which was eventually set up at the Burn Pit. Roebuck had had all the parts for it specially produced at Carron, but not even the expertise of the workers at the famous iron foundry could produce sufficient accuracy to make Watt's idea work. The lack of success was as much a disaster for Roebuck as it was for Watt, because he had helped the inventor obtain his first patent and invested in a two third share in it.

According to Senator Roebuck, 'The water in the mine made better progress than my ancestor and Watt with their steam engine. The mine was a sink hole for money and debts mounted. Roebuck's salt pans at Kinneil also lost money and the doctor failed in an attempt to make soda from the salt. Dr Roebuck withdrew from the Carron Company, sold his interest in a refining works at Birmingham and the sulphuric factory at Prestonpans and borrowed heavily from friends and relatives. But all this was not enough to cover the losses at Kinneil and the creditors took over the estate. They attached so little value to the steam engine patents that they transferred Roebuck's two thirds interest to Matthew Bolton from Birmingham, in exchange for his claim for £1200 against the estate'.

The rest is of course, history. Watt went south to work with Bolton in Birmingham and soon the better made English parts made a success of his new style steam engine. Instead of using it mainly for pumping it was converted to produce rotary power and the cotton mills of Lancashire and Yorkshire owed much of their success to its introduction.

Back at Kinneil while Roebuck's fortune had disappeared he refused to give in. He was retained by the Duke of Hamilton to manage the estate at Kinneil and his lordship's Borrowstounness Coal Workings and Salt Pans and was paid a salary sufficient for the maintenance of himself and his family at Kinneil House from which he also carried on successful farming operations.

All the time however the resourceful doctor was seeking a new opportunity, which would allow him to establish himself in business again and this he found by establishing Scotland's first major commercial pottery down river on the opposite side of Bo'ness at Bridgeness. Just as with the sulphuric acid factory and the foundation of Carron Iron Works, Roebuck planned his new venture with great care. Bridgeness he reckoned was ideal as the site was flat and there were plentiful supplies of coal right on its doorstep to fire the kilns, plenty of collier's wives and daughters to supply cheap female labour and a good little harbour through which raw materials could be imported and many of the finished products shipped to market.

Transport by sea was considered very important by Roebuck as Scottish roads were atrocious; muddy quagmires in winter and deeply rutted dust bowls in summer. He understood clearly that to move china by cart or packhorse would have resulted in much of it being smashed long before it reached its destination. This same problem of bad roads forced Josiah Wedgewood in the Black Country of Staffordshire to build one of England's first canals to provide a cheap means of bringing heavy cargoes of raw materials to his works and an equally safe way to take his fine porcelain to market.

Fortunately at Bridgeness, Roebuck had the Forth flowing right past the site of his pottery. Soon he arranged for his first supplies of clay from Devon and Cornwall, flints from the north of France and special large stones from Argyllshire to grind the flints all to be brought to Bo'ness in a fleet of small sailing ships and his new pottery began production. At first mainly rough ware was turned out and for a time local clay was used to make cheap earthenware pots and bowls for which there was a demand.

After Roebuck's death, the pottery changed hands several times. One owner James Jamieson decided to extend it considerably and widen the range of its products. He brought skilled printers and transferrers north from Staffordshire. Unfortunately the new lines did not prove successful and Jamieson's company became insolvent. Most money was owed to the Redding Coal Company from up on the Braes behind Falkirk. It took over the pottery for a short time until it was able to sell it to Mr John Marshall. When he took over the new owner was greatly disturbed by the bad reputation the potters had in Bo'ness. Local women finding it hard to find husbands are said to have declared, 'We'll, I daursey I'll hae to tak' a potter yet'. The potters were particularly notorious for their drunkenness, drinking often occurring even during working hours.

Marshall and his managers did everything they could to stop this even including locking the pottery gates while production was in progress, but the workers had many ways of smuggling in supplies of beer and spirits. With the assistance of accomplices stationed outside in Main Street, they would pull up bottles tied to window cords. Even the management had to accept that pottery firing was hot, dry, dusty, thirsty work and the custom had grown up that their craftsmen were allowed to send out the apprentices to fetch jugs of water, but often on their return the jugs contained much stronger liquids!

To try to tackle these problems and improve the reputation of the potters, Mr Marshall introduced many paternalistic measures such as a reading room in the manager's house and an annual outing for all his employees. The first passenger train ever to steam out of Bo'ness Station was an excursion special crowded with the potters, their wives and children.

The other big day of the year for the potters was Bo'ness Fair, which had started in 1799 as a miners' march to show that the coal workers had been freed by act of parliament from the thirldom which previously tied them, their wives and families like serfs to the pits where they worked. Soon the other workmen of the town joined in the parade and the potters always dressed up specially for the occasion. They wore white trousers and aprons tied with black ribbons and black tail coats and black tall lum hats and they always carried beautifully made examples of their craft. These included model kilns, model sailing ships and even Union Jack flags made from pottery.

The Bo'ness potters did indeed excel at making specialities and especially a whole range of what became known as chimney piece ornaments of which the famous 'wally dugs' were best known, although they actually produced a whole 'wally' menagerie of animals and birds including golden lions, glossy black cats, and brilliantly coloured parrots. Like the 'wally dugs' these other 'wally' creatures were never faithful in detail to real animals, the potters being much more concerned with making them bright and attractive. 'Wally' was an old Scottish term for the thick coarse china ware of which the 'dugs' were made and it occurs in other uses ranging from 'wally closes', meaning entrances lined with china tiles which led to Glasgow's poshest tenement flats, to 'wallies' as a colloquial term for false teeth!

'Wally dugs' were always in great demand by the local miners' who displayed them proudly on their fireside mantelpieces and the shelves of their wooden kitchen dressers. Whereas fragile Dresden and Wedgewood figurines would have been way beyond their means and in any case out of place in the miners' rows, the solid thick china dogs seemed completely at home and the fact they were glazed allowed any specks of coal dust to be easily wiped or washed off. These 'wally dugs' often became family heirlooms, handed down from mother to eldest daughter for generations, until in the 1930s and 1940s they sadly went out of favour, being considered definitely common and even vulgar. Fortunately the 'wally dugs' are now very much back in favour as fine examples of Scottish Victoriana and are in great demand by American collectors.

'Wally dugs', however, date back much further than the 19th century. Early Egyptian, Persian and Chinese potters all favoured dogs as subjects for their ornaments and J Arnold Fleming in his *Scottish Pottery*, published in 1923, suggested the 'wally dug' design originated among the Moorish potters in Spain as early as the beginning of the 16th century. Merchants returning from the continent probably brought these first examples of 'wally dugs' to Scotland, where they were regarded as a great novelty. Mary Queen of Scots appears to have possessed one because Mr Fleming during his researches discovered in a list of the queen's possessions, drawn up in 1562, an entry which reads, 'ane figure of ane doig in pottery ware'.

It was during the 1800s that the 'wally dugs' with their curly ears like those of a King Charles spaniel really came into vogue. The dogs, which were always modelled in the same squatting position, with the same rather supercilious grins on their flat pug like faces, were always sold in pairs, one facing right and the other left. Where they differed was in their decoration, no two pairs being exactly alike as they were all hand-painted. Among the most popular were the glossy white ones, with their gleaming black or gold eyes, chains and markings.

Wedding jugs were another of the Bo'ness potters specialities. They were tall, white jugs, patterned with red roses or other flowers and with the names of the bride and bridegroom and the date of their marriage beautifully painted in black. Later the wedding jugs were joined on the shelves of the kitchen dresser by smaller china christening mugs. These were little mugs, which like the wedding jugs, were inscribed with all the details of each baby's birth and baptism. Large intricately decorated punch bowls were also a popular Bo'ness product. Most of the bowls bore mottoes such as, 'what art can with the potters' art compare? Forof what we are ourselves, of such, we can make our ware'.

Another favourite novelty produced by the Bo'ness potters were the surprise mugs, which were a popular Victorian party joke. From the outside the attractively decorated mugs looked perfectly innocent and ordinary, but inside lurked a very realistic wee green puddock. The idea was to fill the surprise mug with beer and present it to a guest, who had already had a glass or two and then watch the look of surprised astonishment on his face as the little frog came swimming up to greet him as he downed his drink. Today the surprise mugs are collectors' pieces.

Under Mr Marshall, the Bo'ness pottery flourished and he extended it greatly, building new kilns on flat ground reclaimed from the Forth. It was at this time that Mr Marshall took William McNay into partnership. From then on the McNay family played an increasingly important part in the running of the business. The original pottery in which Dr Roebuck had started the industry was closed in 1889 after the McNays opened their new pottery further along the shore at Bridgeness. By then there were several other smaller potteries in the town including another new one opened in 1878.

In 1911 the potters had to cope with a flood of orders for thousands of coronation mugs, which were issued to pupils at many Scottish schools when King George V was crowned at Westminster Abbey on 22nd June. Smaller orders for similar mugs were placed each year to give to local children at Bo'ness Fair and when architect Bill Cadell of the House of Grange converted the red pantiled stables at Kinneil into the Bo'ness Museum he found a hamper full of them below the rafters of the attic. Appropriately therefore a display of Bo'ness pottery is one of the museum's most attractive exhibits. Sadly no more Bo'ness ware is produced as McNay's Bridgeness Pottery was gutted by fire during the summer of 1963 after the large red brick building had lain empty for three years following the end of production in 1960. It was staffing difficulties which resulted in the closure of the pottery and not lack of orders. During its final years it dealt with large orders for plain white hospital and hotel ware, but the fine sepia and blue and white dinner services decorated with scenes ranging from hunting scenes to the willow pattern and from colonial scenes to horse racing, still to be found in antique shops are a fitting reminder of the quality of the china once produced by the Bo'ness potteries for which Dr Roebuck was responsible.

Roebuck died on 17th July 1794 and lies buried on the shores of the Forth in Carriden graveyard. His gravestone is inscribed in Latin with the words, 'Underneath this tombstone rests no ordinary man. John Roebuck, MD'. His six children brought up at Kinneil House also went on to make their mark in various parts of the world. The oldest and youngest sons, John and Josiah went to Russia, where true to family tradition, they founded a chemical works in St Petersburgh. John and his wife, Anne Livingstone from Bo'ness had a large family, several of whom married into the Russian aristocracy.

Roebuck's second son Benjamin did even better for himself. He emigrated to India, where he served as Paymaster of the Forces of the famous East India Company in Madras, where he is described as living, 'in a state of princely magnificence'. He also still kept an interest in chemistry as a hobby and it is recorded that, 'the natives were inclined to look upon him as something of a wizard, through seeing him perform the simple experiment of making ice in front of a fire which he did by using salt peter and the old lead chamber method'.

David, the doctor's third son, went to China, where he became a successful trader. He married, but died without a direct heir, as he collapsed and passed away suddenly, 'of a chill contracted by sleeping on a marble slab, when very hot'.

Ebenezer, the fourth of the Roebucks, was the acknowledged bad boy of the family. He is described as, 'a high spirited lad', and the tutor whom Roebuck employed to educate his family at Kinneil House had to use his tawse to strap Ebenezer more than his four brothers and sister. Ebenezer resented the fact that he received more whippings than the others and complained that he was, 'harshly and unjustly treated by the schoolmaster'. He therefore ran away from home and made his way to India where he joined his brother Benjamin. There he appeared to settle down, but after a few years returned to Britain, where he developed an interest in a chemical works. It was situated in the London suburb of

A veritable forest of masts and rigging in Bo'ness Dock. John Doherty.

Hounslow, an area which at that time had a very bad reputation for thieves, pickpockets and footpads. He therefore always carried a loaded gun when he travelled to and from the factory. According to Roebuck tradition a highway robber was about to hold him up, when another of the gang shouted, 'That's Roebuck. Don't attack him, for he will surely shoot!' Shortly afterwards he met and fell in love with the delightfully named Zipporah Tickell, who was described as, 'both clever and beautiful'. He married her when she was just sixteen and together they produced six children, three of whom were born in India. India's climate sadly claimed Ebenezer's life, but after returning to this country, Zipporah emigrated again, this time to Canada, There her brother was secretary to Governor General Simcoe and the government gave Zipporah and her children five hundred acres of land near York or Toronto as it later became.

Zipporah's eldest son, John Arthur, subsequently returned to England and became Member of Parliament for Bath, but never lost his interest in Canada for which country he became government agent and represented it in the House of Commons. John Arthur was one of the supporters of the Chartists and one of the main supporters of the Great Reform Act of 1832, which provided all men with the vote for the first time, which at the time was considered a very revolutionary move. Back across the Atlantic the Roebucks have remained one of Canada's most influential families. South of the border in the USA, however, the world famous Sears-Roebuck stores and mail order firm was not founded by one of the descendants of the Bo'ness doctor, but by a cousin from Yorkshire.

Elizabeth, the second youngest of the Roebucks who grew up at Kinneil, later married a Mr Stewart, but whether this was a relative of the Professor Dougald Stewart, author of the famous, *Philosophical Essays*, who later rented Kinneil House, is not known.

The story of Kinneil could not be complete without looking at the ruins of its kirk, which is reached by crossing the little bridge over the Gil Burn. Only the gable wall with its unusual double belfry now stands, but the outline of the church may be traced from its foundations and there are several tombstones the carvings upon which indicate the trades of the people who lived in the little hamlet of Kinneil. The discovery of a large stone Celtic cross, now removed for safe keeping in the cellars of Kinneil house, indicate that Christian worship has taken place on this site even before the building of the church. Despite this there is evidence that black magic and witchcraft were also practised at Kinneil as late as the 17th century with allegations of a plot to kill the infant son of the factor of Kinneil Estate, but that is a matter best dealt with along with all the other Bo'ness witch trials in the later chapter on Carriden and Cuffabouts.

CHAPTER 11
BURGH TOWN ON THE POINT

Bo'ness is short for Barrowstounness, the Burgh Town on the Ness and as its name suggests it sits on a nose of land jutting into the Forth. When it first came into existence Bo'ness was indeed considered to be sticking its nose into other people's business as far as the provost and magistrates of neighbouring Linlithgow were concerned.

They protested vigorously to the Scottish Privy Council about the attempts, by Bo'ness to establish itself as a port, claiming indignantly that it would damage the trade of its harbour less than three miles down river at Blackness. In 1601, however, Bo'ness was officially recognised as a port for the first time, although the place name had been mentioned over a century earlier, interestingly in connection with the skill of one of its sailors. He was Sir David Falconer, second in command to the famous Sir Andrew Wood of Largo in Fife and together on 10th August 1490 in a fierce battle at the mouth of the Forth they routed the English fleet, under the command of Sir Stephen Bull. A contemporary record of the fight describes Sir David as, 'a brave cavalier and skilful mariner of Borrowstounness'.

Bo'ness sailors appear to have been equally expert smugglers because in 1602, only a year after it was officially approved as a port, the Scottish Privy Council ordered its closure again, because of the amount of smuggling taking place. Linlithgow's glee was however short-lived, because within a few years trade at Bo'ness was again flourishing.

Linlithgow protested again, this time about the upstart port's casual disregard for quarantine regulations. With an outbreak of plague raging at the time, the provost and bailies of Linlithgow were fearful it would spread from Bo'ness over the Erngath Hills to their royal and ancient burgh. According to a contemporary account, 'It pleasit God to visite the toun of Borrowstounness with some little infection of the contagious seekness of the pest', but according to the magistrates of Linlithgow it was the Bo'ness port officials' own fault for not enforcing the rules for fear that the delays they caused would loose them trade. In 1645 therefore, the furious Linlithgow magistrates gave orders for, 'the maister of works to erect twa gallases — ane at the East Port, the other at the West Port, and gar hang thereon all persons coming frae Borrowstounness and seeking to enter the toun'. There is no record of any Bo'nessian jouking Lithca's gibbet, perhaps because the Scottish parliament intervened and set up a special committee of local gentlemen to prevent the further spread of the plague and gave these commissioners powers, 'to cause shoot and kill any who come furth of the Burgh of Borrowstounness without our order, under the pain of death'. Again apparently no Bo'nessian decided to put the matter to the test.

Despite Linlithgow's campaigns against Bo'ness it was the latter which was chosen in preference to Linlithgow's outport at Blackness when King James VI decided to export silver ore from God's Blessing, his mine in the Bathgate Hills, to London. The reason for this new royal business for Bo'ness was that the king, who had been in residence in London since the Union of the Crowns in 1603, believed he was being swindled out of the profits from his Linlithgowshire silver mine. By having the ore smelted in London, where he could supervise the operation, instead of at Silver Mill on the banks of the river Avon, James reckoned he could increase the revenue, which he so much required because of what he considered the parsimony of his English parliament. Although James was known as the wisest fool in Christendom, this was a bad decision, because the cost of transporting the heavy ore, rather than the refined silver, outweighed any gain from smelting the silver in London and the royal export business ceased.

Other trade at Bo'ness did, however, continue to grow and at the very start of the 18th century, Linlithgow's worst fears were realised when the customs and excise office was moved from Blackness to Bo'ness. Soon Bo'ness was so busy it was recognised next to Leith as Scotland's most important seaport. It was considered promotion for a customs officer to be transferred from Glasgow to Bo'ness. During the 1700s several titled gentlemen held the post of officer in charge of the customs at Bo'ness.

During this period the harbour was greatly improved and as many as thirty large sailing vessels had Bo'ness as their port of registration. The Bo'ness fleet included seventeen brigantines of between 70 and 170 tons, six of which were under contract to sail

A single motor van was the only vehicle in the early 1920s view of North Street, Bon'ess. On the left can be seen the crowded windows of Douds the Drapers, who each week advertised their bargain prices for ladies' corsets, schoolgirls' fleecy knickers and gentlemens' combinations, on the front page of the Bo'ness Journal.

regularly to and from London once every fourteen days. The other vessels were smaller sloops ranging from 20 to 70 tons, which were generally employed on coasting trade. Exports were mostly made up of coal and slag to the Low Countries and Scandinavia, while imports ranged from timber from the Baltic countries for the local sawmills to clay and flint from Devon and Cornwall for use in the new pottery, which Dr John Roebuck had established at Bridgeness.

The prosperity of Bo'ness was added to even further by the success of its fishing fleet and Bo'nessians became known as 'Garvies', a local name for the millions of tiny herring or sprats which were landed at the port and then salted and exported to Russia and the other Baltic lands, where they were a staple part of the diet.

Towards the end of the 18th century, however, Bo'ness suffered two major setbacks, similar to those which had caused a decrease in Alloa's trade. The freeing of the American colonies ended the re-export business. This meant the disappearance of the tobacco industry and the large stone built tobacco warehouse in Scotland Lane, which still stands and has been converted into the town's impressive public library, was soon empty. The second setback was the opening of the Forth and Clyde Canal, which resulted in a great deal of trade moving to Grangemouth. While this may have given Linlithgow some satisfaction in revenge for Bo'ness originally robbing Blackness of its cargoes, it was particularly galling for Bo'ness as the original plans were for it to be the eastern terminal of the canal and local merchants had actually been confident that it would boost rather than damage their trade.

The stagnation in Britain's merchant trade during the Napoleonic Wars with France at the start of the 19th century was yet another blow as it affected Bo'ness as much as any other British port, especially those on the east coast. This is clearly seen from the customs dues. In 1810 the dues collected at Bo'ness amounted to £30,486. By the time the war ended in 1815, Bo'ness collected scarcely a tenth of that, the returns for that year coming to only £3,835.

Even after the defeat of Napoleon at Waterloo trade was slow to revive and by 1839 the Bo'ness fleet was down to fourteen vessels and most of these were small. Around the middle of the century the opening of iron foundries and more timber yards and sawmills together with the coming of the railway all helped improve matters, but as with Alloa it was the industrial revolution's demand for coal and in turn that industries need for pit-props, which brought prosperity back to Bo'ness.

The pit-prop trade was actually invented in Bo'ness by the young cashier at the Grange Colliery, George C Stewart, who later went on to become the town's provost. The enterprising Stewart realised that with the sinking of deeper pits and the change from the old Scottish stoop and room method of mining to the more modern and efficient long wall method, there was a new demand for wooden props to support the roofs of the mine workings in place of the inefficient stoops or stacks which had previously been left in place to do the job. At first the props were cut to size by the miners at the start of each shift, but Stewart recognised that this was wasteful of both time and timber. He went into partnership therefore with a Glasgow business man, Mr James Love and together they set about importing ready cut props in a variety of sizes, lengths and diameters, from the forests of Russia and Scandinavia. Soon they realised they could make even more profits by buying their own ships, including the famous *Lovart*, which they proudly named after themselves.

Soon Bo'ness was surrounded by a veritable forest of pit-props stacked high all the way from Kinneil to Carriden and it was said it was possible to smell Bo'ness before you saw it, because of the sweet smell of resin oozing from the props as the woodyard workers including many women, ripped the bark from the tree trunks, before they were loaded into railway wagons for delivery to collieries all across central Scotland. Pit-props became so synonymous with Bo'ness that it became known as 'Pitpropalis' or 'Proptown' for short. The latter was the title local poet Hope A Thomson chose for one of his works, which read:

The clang of busy hammers fills the air,
the circling saw is moaning in the mill,
Piercing the thick, black night a ghostly glare
Lurid arises from the smoking kiln.

A rail-bound shore, a maze of masts and ropes,
The rumbling rush and crash of landing coal,
And miles of laden trucks and stacks of props,
Strong labour's echoes, loud as thunder roll.

The spacious kiln is full with safars lined,
Which half clad Kilnmen up the ladders bear
In tanks the mighty stones revolve which grind
The brittle flint that glosses o'er the ware.

Long may the Proptown hammers clang! Long may
Its ships bring forest treasures o'er the seas!
Long may the workers fight their honest way,
And in the fight enjoy prosperity!

Many of the Bo'ness industries Hope A Thomson pictures so vividly in his poem from the potteries to the sawmills and the propyards all found suitable flat and spacious sites thanks to the enterprise of one local family, the Cadells of Grange. Originally from Cockenzie in East Lothian as already mentioned in the chapter on Carron Iron Works, they moved upriver to Bo'ness as a result of their interest in Carron. At the same time they saw an opportunity to increase their profits from the ironworks by supplying Carron with coal it needed to feed its hungry furnaces. The Duke of Hamilton already owned all the collieries to the west of Bo'ness, so the Cadells turned their attention to sinking pits to the east of the harbour out along the coast to Blackness and Carriden where the carboniferous coal bearing measures dipped below the Forth and crossed to Fife.

With so many pits producing coal, the Cadells found they had a problem of how to cope with the resultant waste and rather than let it pile up in bings as it was doing at Slaghill at Kinneil and at the other Hamilton owned pits to the west they decided to put it to work to reclaim acres of land from the Forth. As a geologist Henry M Cadell used his expertise to construct a series of lagoons into which the pit waste was dumped. At high tide the waste was supplemented by silt brought in by the Forth and a clever series of barrages trapped this as the river ebbed. At first the new acres which emerged from the Forth were not firm enough for building, but were ideal as space for the expanding the timber and pit-prop yards.

It was the enterprising Cadells who were also responsible for building one of Scotland's few windmills, the tower of which still stands on its little hilltop site overlooking the Forth at Bridgeness. At one time it was thought the windmill was built specially to provide power to pump the river water out of the family's coal pits, where flooding was always a problem, but there is now doubt about this and it appears more likely it ground the grain from the Cadell farms. In any case wind power was soon made redundant by the coming of steam engines.

Rather than demolish the mill tower, the Cadells decided to utilise it to pursue another of their interests, astronomy. The sails were stripped from the tower and on its roof was erected the largest telescope ever seen in Scotland. Costing £1,000 the six-inch telescope was shipped north in pieces from London. The problem then was how to put it all together again. It was decided to summon help from an English astronomer called Clarke to re-assemble the telescope and show them how to operate it. According to his original contract Mr Clarke was to stay at Bridgeness Tower for only six months, but in the end he stayed for almost thirty years and became one of the town's most colourful characters.

From a time early in his stay at the tower, when his servant carelessly lost a half sovereign gold coin, he insisted on doing his own shopping. On these daily forays into town he always wore a tail silk hat, which made him a figure of great interest to the Bo'ness bairns, who believed that in some strange way this very peculiar man from Bridgeness Tower controlled the local weather.

Bridgeness Tower dominates this picture, taken looking north-east down the slope of Philpingston Road. The Tower was originally a windmill, then an observatory. It is now an award winning private house.

'What kind o' day will it be the morn?' they cried whenever he loomed in sight and he always had a ready answer for them. On Sundays, Mr Clarke did not stroll into Bo'ness, but instead sauntered forth in the opposite direction from the tower east along the shore of the Forth to neighbouring Carriden Parish Church. There his frequent bursts of laughter often interrupted the minister,

105

even during prayers, much to the consternation of the other parishioners.

When Mr Clarke died, the telescope was sold to the Astronomer Royal in London and Bridgeness Tower's four large round rooms were then converted into four separate houses. The best houses in Bo'ness for lazy housewives as the local joke put it, because there were no corners for the dust to gather. Four different families continued to occupy the four levels of the tower with their grandstand view of Bridgeness Miners' Welfare Club's two tennis courts and bowling green, until well into the 1950s. Around this time during a severe thunder storm a bolt of lightening struck and demolished the little turret which had until then graced the roof of the tower and shortly afterwards each of the families left their unusual home. For a time the historic old tower lay empty. The Cadell family offered it to the town as a setting for the proposed local heritage museum, but while its large well lit rooms would have been ideal for such a purpose, its one spiral stair made fire regulations for the admission of the public impossibly expensive to comply with. Just as it looked as if Bridgeness Tower might well be demolished thus robbing the area of one of its best known and loved landmarks, Mr William Cadell used his knowledge as an architect with a practice concentrating on the restoration of historic buildings, from castles to cottages, to restore the tower and make it the centre piece for an attractive small traditional housing development.

Another well-known Bo'ness industry for which Bridgeness Tower's balustraded roof top often provided a spectacular bird's eye view were the shipbreaking yards of P and W McLellan. The main yard was situated almost directly below the tower at the old Bridgeness Harbour, while the other was sited just along the shore of the Forth at Carriden. No matter at which a ship was beached, the sight was breath taking. For sad though it always was to see a vessel completing her last voyage, it was nevertheless also very exciting to see a ship arrive to be scrapped at either Bridgeness or Carriden. For unlike the procedure at other shipbreakers, such as at Faslane on the Gare Loch on the Clyde or further down the Forth at Wards of Inverkeithing, it was not simply a matter of the old ship slipping quietly alongside the quay and ringing finished with engines. Instead at Bo'ness it meant her captain's last instruction to his engine room being, 'full steam ahead'. Then with

Corbiehall, named after the Hill of the Crows, was the scene of the execution of the warlock, John Craw, and the five Bo'ness witches. The belfry of the original 17th-century Bo'ness Parish Church and its Victorian replacement on top of the Pan Braes are both shown. The old church became the Star Cinema, and queues of patrons waiting for seats used to form in the graveyard.

one of the local Forth pilots, of whom Jackie Findlater, Bill Muir and Tom Roberts were considered most accurate, on the bridge to provide detailed knowledge of river conditions, the ship steadied herself for her final voyage. Then once in line with the breakers yard's tallest crane and often with her complete crew still lining the decks she began her final suicidal dash for the shore. For a moment it always looked to the crowds of spectators gathered at vantage points such as the top of Bridgeness Tower, as if the ship, whether she be naval vessel, oil tanker, cargo ship or passenger liner, must inevitably speed on into the line of cottages, which line the shore road. Then suddenly there was always a tremendous crash as she grounded fast, usually only feet from the spot marked out for her by the breaker's men.

All the drama of life at the Bridgeness and Carriden ship-breaking yards is vividly caught in Bo'ness author Bill Sleath's 1920s novel *Breakers of Ships*. Although long out of print, copies may be borrowed from the town's public library.

While Bo'ness was latterly remembered as a place where ships ended their lives at the scrap yard, two centuries earlier it was also a the site of two ship building yards. The yards belonged to

Thomas Boag and Robert Hart. Hart later went into partnership with a Mr Shaw and it was at Shaw and Hart's that Henry Bell, who later gained fame through his invention of the world's first practical sea going steamship, served his apprenticeship. Although Bell commissioned John Wood of Port Glasgow to build *The Comet* on the Clyde, he clearly had great respect for the expertise of the Bo'ness shipbuilders, where he had learned his trade, because it was to it that he brought his new vessel, through the Forth and Clyde Canal, for her first annual overhaul.

Rather ironically, the success of Bell's steamship, sounded the death knell for the Bo'ness shipbuilding industry because with the coming of steam power and iron hulled vessels, the Clyde became Scotland's major shipbuilding centre. Prior to then in the 17th and 18th century Bo'ness built many fine sailing ships including several in the 1690s for the ill fated Darien Scheme.

Most of the Bo'ness ships were, however, built for local owners, best known being John Anderson. Anderson became so successful, rich and powerful that he became known as the uncrowned king of Bo'ness. In 1859 he was honoured by a visit from the Duke of Hamilton and his wife, the German Princess Marie of Baden, youngest daughter of the reigning Grand Duke of Baden and a cousin of the late Emperor Napoleon III of France. Anderson entertained them to cake and wine aboard one of his Greenland whalers, which was berthed in the harbour.

As well as being a successful merchant, Anderson also became the town's first banker. Amongst those to whom he lent money was schoolmaster Henry Gudge. Gudge was the master in charge of the school at the East Partings in South Street, which was one of the largest in Bo'ness, but despite his income from his fees he got seriously into debt and could not repay Anderson. After several warnings Anderson evicted the schoolmaster from his home in Corbiehall. Gudge was very bitter about this and resolved to have his revenge on Anderson while at the same time making himself very rich.

From the conversations of his pupils, Gudge knew that Anderson paid one of the boys every Saturday to carry his surplus funds the seven miles to Falkirk. This Gudge decided was exactly the chance he required. On the following Saturday morning Gudge set out for Falkirk, leaving half an hour before his pupil always departed, but knowing that if he walked slowly the boy would

The unusual design of Bo'ness Town Hall was intended from the distance to make it appear circular. The odd design made it necessary to have two clocks, and both never seemed to show the same time! It was officially opened in 1904, and the semi-circular projection at the far end housed the reading room of the town's library, gifted to it by the steel magnate, Andrew Carnegie.

soon catch up on him. This the boy did at the Crawyett, where the last of the houses on the outskirts of Bo'ness gave way to open countryside. The dominie immediately hailed him and kept the boy talking for about half a mile as they walked on along the shore of the Forth. All the time Gudge kept his eye on the bulging money bag. Suddenly the schoolmaster pretended he could see a hare in one of the fields below Kinneil Woods. The boy, of course, could see nothing and so Gudge offered to hold the bag for a moment so that he could scramble through the hedge to see if the hare was still in sight.

As soon as the boy was on the other side of the hedge, Gudge ran off with the money and by the time the boy gave up his quest for the imaginary hare, the schoolmaster was out of sight. After waiting for some time expecting his teacher to reappear, the full meaning of what had happened slowly dawned and the boy made his way back into Bo'ness, terrified to confess what had happened to Mr Anderson.

The hue and cry was raised at once, but no trace could be found of the erring teacher. A visit to the lodgings he had been forced to move to since being deprived of his house by Anderson, proved he had taken all his valuables with him. With more than £300 at stake, a large sum indeed in those days, Mr Anderson decided to issue a reward of £25 for any information on the whereabouts of Henry Gudge. The reward posters were printed and published in Edinburgh and it was there a girl, who had once attended Gudge's school in Bo'ness chanced to read one. This was to prove Gudge's undoing because the girl immediately recalled that only a few days before, she had been surprised to see her former teacher emerging rather unsteadily from a pub in Bristo Street. She had not spoken to him because she had no love for the schoolmaster, whose twin thonged tawse had repeatedly stung her palms as she had tried to master the intricacies of reading. But now she was glad she had learned her lessons, for thanks to Gudge's teaching she could read the details of the reward and wasted no time in claiming it. She ran to the High Street where she contacted the well-known Edinburgh detective McLevy. Together they made their way to the pub, where they found Gudge seated with a bottle of whisky before him. While the girl watched, McLevy summoned assistance and soon Gudge was under arrest. When he was searched, three ginger beer bottles were found in his coat pocket. All three were stuffed full of pound notes. When counted they totalled £180.

Henry Gudge was subsequently tried at the High Court and sentenced to be transported to Van Diemen's Land, as Tasmania was then known, for twenty years. Towards the end of the period he wrote one letter to a former friend in Bo'ness, stating he hoped, having paid his penalty in full, to return soon to the town. But shortly afterwards he died in Australia in 1859.

Ridding Bo'ness of one dishonest teacher was not John Anderson's only contribution to education in his home town. Much more importantly he gave the money to erect the town's first purpose built secondary school. Known as the Anderson Academy it stood on the east side of Providence Brae and its opening was marked with full Masonic ceremony as John Anderson was a leading member of this organisation. Bo'ness Academy has subsequently moved twice, first at the beginning of this century to the stylish neo-classical building in Stewart Avenue, which is now occupied by the pupils of Bo'ness Public School and then in 1931 to its present Academy Road site on the southern outskirts. The original Victorian building was demolished following a fire in the

1960s. While it is perhaps a pity that Bo'ness Academy has not kept its benefactor's name as part of its title as in the case of Bell Baxter High School in Coupar and the Nicholson Institute in Stornoway, John Anderson still has a small influence on education in the town, through the Anderson Trust and its membership of the West Lothian Education Trust, which provides bursaries and travel grants for local pupils.

Apart from maintaining his interest in education, the Anderson Trust members still meet regularly as he instructed in his will when he died in 1870, to administer his bequests to Bo'ness pensioners. Although the quarterly bequests have been increased from the £4, which he decreed to keep in line with the present day cost of living, his Trustees still only receive five shillings (25p) for each meeting they attend and high tea at a local restaurant. In return they dutifully look after Anderson's property interests including the shops on the south side of South Street and also ensure that his family's tombstones in the old graveyard on the Wynd and his memorial at the entrance to the cemetery in Dundas Street are cleaned and kept in good order.

Anderson's memorial bears the Bo'ness coat of arms depicting a ship under full sail and the Latin motto, *Sine Metu*, 'Without Fear', which sums up how this remarkable Victorian entrepreneur lived his whole life and so it seems appropriate that one of his trustees is always a representative from the town's Sea Box Society. The General United Sea Box Society of Borrowstounness to give it its full title, is an even older Bo'ness institution than the Anderson Trust as it was established in 1634 and has operated ever since. It takes its name from the wooden sea chest into which the masters and crews of all Bo'ness ships agreed to put a tenth of their profits and wages after every successful voyage. The money was then to be used to provide what must surely be the earliest form of welfare state in the country, with a carefully detailed scale of sickness benefits and pensions, not just for the seamen but for their wives and families and on occasions for other needy folk, not even necessarily always from Bo'ness.

To ensure the funds of the Sea Box were scrupulously honestly administered the sea chest was 'double lockit' and no one member ever had the keys for both of the massive iron locks. In the rules it was laid down that the box could only be opened in the presence of two of the skippers and later the Box Master had also to be present.

In addition to money from successful voyages the Sea Box's funds were boosted by giving surplus amounts known as light money to senior captains to invest as they saw fit on the exchanges of the foreign cities which they visited on their trips abroad. The Bo'nessians were obviously shrewd businessmen as well as good skippers and the money in the Sea Box grew steadily. From the outset the business of the society was carried out immaculately and all details of payments from the funds were carefully recorded. Most were routine handouts of pensions to old sailors or their widows, sickness benefits and grants to children whose fathers had drowned at sea. Not all payments were however to members or their dependents and some of these are particularly interesting. Examples include:

1647...Given to five poor Frenchmen of St Maloos, taken by Ostenders.

1649...Given to a distressed seaman, robbed by Irish Men of Warre, to help him to his friends.

1702...To William Gray, prisoner from Dunkirk, being a seaman belonging to Dublin, by order.

1703...To one poor seaman, wanting ane hand.

1703...Payd to a shipbroken man of Pittenweem, by order.

1705...To two shipbroken men who had come from Rotterdam, both belonging to Dublin.

1753...By cash to a dumb sailor having his tongue cut out by the Algerines, assested by the Consul of Leghorn.

It would be interesting to know whether these foreign ports helped Bo'ness sailors in similar cases of distress but this is not recorded. The generosity of the Bo'ness Sea Box to other non members is however well detailed with one entry promising, 'free education for all bairns of this burgh' and another recording the payment of all the timber, slates and other building materials required to build the parish church in Corbiehall, on the site now occupied by the Star Cinema, when it moved there in the 17th century. The Sea Box even provided a fine wooden pulpit shipped all the way from Amsterdam.

In true old Scottish fashion Sea Box members were always concerned that they should have a decent funeral. The Sea Box therefore not only provided a grant to pay for the costs but also arranged all the details. When a death occurred the Society's own

Bo'ness Sea Box Scoiety members gathered in front of Rondebush, the home of John Cochrane, the bearded gentleman seated at the extreme left of the front row. He named the house after a suburb in Cape Town, after returning from South Africa to run the family's engineering business in Bo'ness. His grandson, Bill Cochrane, continues the family's long connection with the society, which he served as president for 27 years. The president is now Dr John Callendar. W Cochrane.

bellman walked slowly through the streets tolling the society's bronze bell. Every few steps he paused to solemnly announce, 'All brethren and sisters, I let ye to wit, there is a brother departed at the pleasures of the almighty, called...All those that come to the burial come at two of the clock. The corpse is at...' Later the bellman walked in front of the funeral procession in which the corpse was carried in a mortcloth again provided by the Sea Box, in those days when a wooden coffin was a luxury which few could afford. As the body slid into the grave the mortcloth was removed and re-used at future funerals and this linen shroud is still among the society's treasured relics, which are on display at the Bo'ness Museum at Kinneil.

The museum also includes a small display on the Bo'ness whalers who enjoyed two particular periods of prosperity in the late 18th and mid 19th century. By the latter time the government was so eager to maximise the supply of oil for the industrial revolution, which was then at its prosperous height. To encourage this it offered a bounty to all whalers which sailed by a certain date each April.

As a result all the Bo'ness Arctic ships set sail on the same day, which was always a big occasion in the town. Wives and sweethearts lined the quaysides, knowing they would not see their loved

113

ones again until September. The crowds of Bo'nessians were swollen by people from neighbouring towns, 'Black Bitches' as the natives of Linlithgow were known even crossing the Flints, to see the whaling fleet set sail. There were cheers as the members of the crews went aboard all rigged out in new uniforms of thick knitted woollen jerseys, black waterproofs, fisherman like bonnets and high leather sea boots, oiled with goose grease and made specially by the Linlithgow snabs. It was said the Bo'ness whalers deliberately never learned to swim, because they knew if they fell into the icy Arctic waters that would only prolong the agony, and they often jested that the Linlithgow cobblers unknowingly did them a favour because their heavy boots guaranteed they would drown faster!

A special cheer always went up upon the arrival of the harpooners, because it was upon their skill and accuracy that the success of the whole voyage depended. Once they were aboard the whalers were ready to put to sea, which they did with a bang, as they fired off the little cannons they all carried, mounted on their sterns.

This was the signal for the crowd to break and run up the steep braes behind Bo'ness to watch as *The Home Castle*, *The Jean*, *The Ratler*, and *The Success*, which was always known as 'The Lucky Success' sailed away out of sight down the Forth. Each whaler was of around 300 tons.

The Bo'ness fleet stayed together, as did the boats from Leith, Burntisland, Kirkcaldy, Dundee, Montrose, Aberdeen, Peterhead, Banff and Kirkwall, until they reached the hunting grounds off the Faroes and Iceland. Once there it was every ship for herself and a constant watch was kept from high in the crow's-nest on the mainmast in the hope of making the first kill.

As soon as the shout of 'Whale Ho!' rang out the mother ship launched her six or eight small rowing boats, which to this day are known as 'whalers'. Each was crewed by four oarsmen, a coilsman and the harpooner. While the harpooner took up his position in the bows the coilsman sat in the stern, where it was his duty to make certain the line attached to the eight foot long wooden harpoon with its barbed metal tip ran free, when the harpooner launched his lethal weapon.

These primitive harpoons, made for the Bo'ness whalers by the local blacksmith at Kinneil, did not have any explosive charge in their tips, so it was necessary to be within very close range before they had any effect on the sixty to eighty foot whales which were often caught. Usually more than one strike was necessary and there was always the danger that the furiously thrashing injured whale would capsize the small boat, as it tried desperately to escape by diving under the nearest ice flow. It was known for a wounded whale to tow a small boat for several miles and this the Bo'ness men called 'sledging down the school brae' as they sped across the ice strewn waters.

They knew when their catch was exhausted and near to death when the whale spouted blood. 'There's a fire in her lum', was the cry as they closed in for the final kill, which meant another sign of the whale's tail etched at the side of that day's date in their ships's log.

When a harpooner was successful in killing a whale all the other small boats raced to help him tow his catch alongside. Then no matter how exhausted the crew were, they quickly swapped their sea boots for boots with metal spikes in the soles and scrambled onto the whale's back to start what was known as 'the flensing'. For they knew the carcass would only float for a limited time and it was essential to obtain all the vital blubber and bones, which also had a commercial value.

The fatty blubber was cut up into blocks about the size of large bricks and stored in the whaler's holds. Unlike their Dutch and Norwegian rivals the Scottish whalers never appear to have tried to boil the blubber while in the Arctic, always preferring to ship it home to the refineries in each of their home ports.

In Bo'ness there were two of these early refineries, one half way up on the east side of the School Brae and the other where Davidson's and later Livingston's garage was situated on the Wynd, just below Tidings Hill, which got its name as it was from this vantage point that the wives, girlfriends and the old retired seaman of the town made their daily pilgrimages when the whalers were expected home.

The problem was that not all returned, because for those which had had a poor season with few catches and a marked absence of flukes inked in the log, there was always the great temptation to stay another and then another day in the northern waters and be trapped in the ice. Although all the Bo'ness whalers had their bows strengthened to resist the pressure of the ice, it was hard to break free once the ice formed and the prospect of a winter spent in the freezing darkness of the Arctic was a grim one, with logs recording men reduced to catching and eating rats, ice forming on the pillows on their bunks and frozen ink making it impossible to write anymore.

For those who did make it back safely however, the prizes were good. The largest cargo of blubber landed in Scotland was brought ashore by the *Resolution* of Peterhead, which caught forty four whales in 1814. When their blubber was processed it produced £10,000 worth of oil, a great sum in the early 19th century and to this was added another £1,000 from an auction of bones. The long flexible whale bones were always in demand from furniture makers, for manufacturing into waist pinching stays for fashionable ladies and even more painful for making long leather covered instruments of corporal punishment called 'pandybats', which were used in Irish schools instead of canes or straps, the term 'pandy' coming from the Latin command *Pande Manum* meaning, 'hold out your hand'.

The one product the Scottish whalers never marketed was whale meat, because they lacked refrigeration, despite all the ice around them in their faraway hunting grounds.

Whaling from Bo'ness came to an end for three reasons. Firstly, ironically, was the very successful seasons enjoyed during the 1860s, which left fewer whales for future years. Secondly during the same period the superior products of James 'Paraffin' Young's West Lothian shale oil industry came onto the market. Thirdly and most spectacularly the larger of the two Bo'ness refineries on the Wynd caught fire. The blaze broke out on a freezing cold winter night, when there was no water available to fight it. It spread rapidly and several of the barrels of oil exploded, sending a river of flaming oil flowing down the Wynd.

Possibly because of the refinery fire, Bo'ness never experimented with steam whalers, which sailed from Dundee and some other Scottish ports in the 1870s and which despite the old hands predictions that the noise of their engines and propellers would warn away the whales did succeed in increasing catches for a while by venturing into more distant waters such as the Davis Straits and Melville Bay, which the sailing ship skippers had considered too far away and too dangerous. Nor did the Bo'ness whalers ever venture to the Antarctic to which three Dundee vessels first sailed in 1893 and in which Salvesen of Leith maintained a Scottish interest until the 1960s, thus incidentally resulting in Edinburgh Zoo having the largest penguin collection in captivity and even making penguins a Scottish export!

In Bo'ness a few links with whaling lingered on into this century with a whale's jaw bone forming an arch over a garden gate on the Wynd and houses in the Waggon Row overlooking the harbour having their living rooms on the first floor and their bedrooms on the ground floor because they were the homes of the whaling fleet skippers and after the long summers at sea they insisted during their winters in port in still going down to their bunks at night.

Now oil aplenty comes to Bo'ness, without having to risk the hazards of the Arctic to get it, because the North Sea pipeline comes ashore from under the Forth in the town and of course far more of its inhabitants now earn their living from the oil industry than ever did in the days of the whalers, as they work at the British Petroleum oil refinery at Grangemouth, in its related industries or out on the rigs in the North Sea. Perhaps these latter still more than any other folk in the town keep up the brave traditions of the whalers of old, because like them the risks they run from flying out by helicopter to life on the rigs themselves and from the risk of explosions to the ferocity of winter gales, are not inconsiderable.

CHAPTER 12
CARRIDEN, CUFFABOUTS AND CROOKIES

Carriden means the fort on the hill and may well take its name from the most easterly of the Roman fortifications on the line of Antonine's Wall. It is certainly likely that Roman supply galleys docked here as well as up river at Bridgeness Harbour at the actual point where the wall reached the river. It is believed that the civilian settlement which grew up around the end of the wall stretched east along the shore of the Forth at this point, but any chance of excavating this site was destroyed when during the 19th century there was massive dumping of pit waste to reclaim more acres from the river.

The pit waste came, of course, from the local collieries and it was coal, which brought Carriden its first mentions in historic records. Carriden is indeed claimed to be one of the first places in Scotland where coal was mined. The first miners were the monks of Holyrood in Edinburgh. They received a tithe from local land-owner William de Vipont, entitling them to all the coal they could gather from these lands beside the Forth, from where they could ship the coal down river to the nearest point to their monastery, thus avoiding the problem of moving heavy loads any further than absolutely necessary overland.

Later in 1291 more monks from across the river from Dunfermline Abbey were also given the right to dig for coal. Yet over one hundred years later in other parts of Europe the value of coal was apparently still unknown. For during the reign of King James I in the year 1435 Aeneas Sylvius, who later became Pope Pius II, rode through the Lothians and wrote in his journal that he was amazed to see, 'the poor, who almost in a state of nakedness begged at the church doors, depart with joy in their faces on receiving stones as alms'. Later in another account of his visit to Scotland the future Pope wrote, 'A sulphurous stone dug from the earth is used by the people as fuel'.

At first mining at Carriden took the form of 'ingaun e'es', slanting shafts which dug into surface seams of coal. The 'ingaun e'es' or 'in-going eyes' took their name from the fact that by night the miners' candles lit the hill along the riverside like little winking eyes. Later as the outcrops and surface seams were worked out, the first shafts were sunk. These were known as bell pits as they consisted simply of a shaft and the workings around its base and thus resembled the shape of an old fashioned wooden handled bell. As soon as the coal around the immediate base of the shaft was exhausted, it was simpler to sink another shaft nearby, rather than go to the trouble to dig underground passages.

Thanks to the homes which the miners built for themselves Carriden, like Kinneil to the west, became a parish long before the 17th-century existence of Bo'ness. There have in fact been no fewer than three Carriden Churches, two on the shores of the Forth at the foot of Carriden Brae and the first higher up the hill in the grounds of what is now Carriden House. Stretching back over so many years the Carriden Kirk Session records contain many items of interest from its attempts to ensure a good education for every bairn in its parish to orders to its beadle to do his duty as church officer and birch any delinquent boys.

While it was the errant boys of the parish who felt the correction of corporal chastisement, the misbehaving girls and women of Carriden were actually in much greater danger, because the members of the kirk session carried out regular witch-hunts and the penalty for witchcraft was death! One of the earliest cases involved the summoning of Margaret Thomson, who was ordered to appear before the session to answer a charge of using, 'magical arts in burning of a corn riddle to find out some money she wanted'. To make matters worse this fire had occurred on the Sabbath.

More serious, during the 1640s a Commission of Gentlemen found six women guilty of witchcraft at Carriden and all of them were sentenced to be strangled and then have their bodies burned at the stake.

At Hallowe'en in the year 1679 the action in the witch-hunt moved into Bo'ness. Rumours of dreadful bloodcurdling deeds practised at dead of night swept through the town. This time a warlock was amongst those arrested along with five women accused of witchcraft. He was appropriately named John Craw and it is intriguing to wonder whether being named after this large black bird contributed to his evil image. The five women arrested for alleged witchcraft were Bessie Vicar, Margaret Hamilton,

Margaret Pringle, Annable Thomsone and a second Margaret Hamilton. All were accused of having sold both their bodies and souls to the Devil.

Stories spread rapidly about how the six had all meet with the De'il at the Muirstane above Carriden on the unlucky night of 13th October and of how they had danced around the stone, while Auld Nick had skirled on the pipes. Worse still it was claimed they had plotted to kill the baby son of Andrew Mitchell, the estate factor at Kinneil.

As the Bo'ness folk crowded the streets, Craw and his five female companions, all of whom were widows, were arrested and led to the thick stone-walled Tolbooth in South Street, where they were all imprisoned to await trial. The charges against them were considered so serious that the Scottish Privy Council in Edinburgh ordered eight of the most prominent gentlemen in Linlithgowshire as West Lothian was then known, to act as commissioners and try the case.

At last, less than a week before Christmas, on 19th December, all was ready for the trial to begin. The commissioners rode into town. The accused were brought from their cells into the crowded court to hear the evidence of their townsfolk against them. On that cold winter morning the proceedings began with the reading of the indictment. It stated, 'Yee cand ilk ane of you ar indytted and accyused that whereas the cryme of witchcraft is declared to be ane horrid abominable and capital cryme, punishable with the paines of death and the confiscation of moveables, nevertheless it is of veritee that you have committed and are gwyltie of the saidd cryme of witchcraft in so far as ye have entered into paction with the Devil, the enemie of your salvation and have renounced our blessed Lord and saviour and your baptisme and have given yourselves, both soulles and bodies to the Devil'.

After they were all accused of having had several meetings with the Devil, the individual crimes of Craw and of each of the five women were solemnly read out. Annable Thomsone was declared to have first met the devil while walking home from Linlithgow to Bo'ness, when he approached her in the 'lykeness oof ane black man'. Dear knows what the Race Relations Board would have to say nowadays! Perhaps the man really did exist and was a coloured sailor or even an escaped slave trying to reach the port at Bo'ness, but whatever it must have been a very unusual and therefore highly suspicious occurrence in 17th-century Scotland.

Margaret Hamilton in her turn was accused of having met the Devil in Bo'ness itself because she was alleged to have first met him at the town well in the Market Square and to have later invited him to her home on several occasions. There, it was alleged, he had drunk ale and had paid her with a five merk gold piece, which she had later claimed turned into a worthless wee stone.

More evidence was led that when Margaret Pringle promised to follow Auld Nick, he had actually shaken her right hand so hard that for eight days it had been, 'grievously pained' until the De'il returned and shook it again, whereupon it was immediately cured.

As the day wore on the courtroom with its low ceiling and its small windows became darker and darker and when the tapers and candles were eventually lit they sent ghostly shadows flickering up the white washed walls. At last by late afternoon, all of the evidence, such as it was, had been heard and the Commissioners retired. When they returned to the courtroom it was to announce they had found all six accused guilty of witchcraft.

Immediately the verdict was given, amid the shrieks and wails of the prisoners, the spokesman for the Commissioners pronounced sentence upon the miserable six, that they were all to be publicly burned to death for their evil deeds. Carefully and methodically the clerk to the court wrote down the instructions of the Commissioners about how the horrific execution was to be carried out. All six were to be taken, 'to the ordinary place of execution', and there, 'on the 23rd of December, between the hours of two and four in the afternoon' they were to be, 'wirried at a stake till they be dead and thereafter to have their bodies burnt to ashes'.

The Bailie Principal of the Regalitie of Borrowstounness and his Deputies were at once instructed to make all the necessary arrangements for the mass execution and to make certain it was carried out in all its dreadful detail. Thus four days later the five witches and the warlock, John Craw, were led down from their cells in the old Tolbooth for the last time. Watched by a silent crowd, including many of their neighbours, they were marched west along South Street and through Corbiehall to the flat stretch of ground on the shore of the Forth to the west of the town.

There the six stakes had been set up in readiness and fires were soon lit. One by one the six had their throats rung by the town hangman, before their bodies were consumed by the leaping flames. By the time the pale winter sun had dipped below the Ochil Hills on that December afternoon, only two days before Christmas, the executions were all over, the fires had burnt themselves down to their glowing embers; justice had been done and Bo'ness was rid of its poor, innocent witches.

Twenty five years later in 1704 another witch-hunt occurred this time once again at Carriden, where the kirk session ordered Anna Wood to appear before it. The first witness was a sailor called Robert Nimmo. He declared that on the previous Monday evening at about seven o'clock when it was dark he had been coming home from Linlithgow when he encountered six mewing black cats. They followed him all the way over the Erngath Hills until he came to Sir Walter Seton's home at Park Dyke at Northbank. There they suddenly all changed into black-clad wailing women. One of whom he recognised as the accused, Anna Wood, screamed and threatened to kill him. In front of his eyes the women then all equally suddenly changed into black birds and flapped round him menacingly until they turned back into women again. The women again included Anna Wood and she along with the others accompanied him down the hill as far as the House of Grange, where they all vanished, just as suddenly as they had first appeared.

Other seamen then gave evidence that Anna had appeared aboard their ship. The captain of the vessel, James Steadmen, also stated that Anna had even appeared before him in his cabin when the ship was docked in Holland and that shortly afterwards the ship's boy had been lost overboard.

Whether Anna would have been found guilty of the lad's murder by witchcraft we will never know, because she apparently decided not to trust in the wisdom of the Carriden Session, but managed instead to escape and flee, before they could reach their decision.

She was probably very wise, because the Carriden Session had in the past been known to convict a woman wrongly of witchcraft. The women in this case was Isobel Wilson and luckily for her the session imprisoned her rather than executing her, because after a spell in prison the Scottish Privy Council reviewed her case and ordered her release!

It was not until 1736 that the old act against witchcraft was abolished and the death penalty for 'traffickers with Satan' was replaced by a maximum sentence of one year in prison and three months in the pillory. This penalty was to apply to all who practised the occult arts or pretended to tell fortunes or used the supernatural to recover stolen goods.

The reduced sentence seems also to have reduced the Carriden Session's interest in witchcraft, but its records still went on to contain occasional intriguing incidents in the life of the parish, none more so than when Sarah Small, schoolmistress of the Grangepans dame school was ordered to appear before it. Miss Small was accused of brawling in the street with her neighbour Margaret Robertson. It must indeed have been quite a fight because it was alleged that after Mrs Robertson had called the teacher a 'witch thief', Miss Small had hit her so hard in the face that it knocked her to the ground, where she proceeded to administer the kind of thrashing usually reserved for the worst of her pupils. She was found guilty and warned about her future conduct.

Evidence of two other schools in the parish of Carriden can still be found at the top of Carriden Brae in the model village of Muirhouses or 'the Murrays' as it is usually known locally. Like the village itself the school on the corner of the little square and the sewing school for the girls at the entrance to the estate, on the brae, were established by the Hopes of Carriden House. This paternalistic approach was especially typical of Admiral Sir James Hope, who had previously adopted a similar approach to the sailors on his ships.

Sir James was born at Carriden House, which is now a luxurious guest house owned by the Barkhouse family, in 1808. His father, Sir George, was also an admiral, who at the time was Commander in Chief of the British Fleet in the Baltic fighting against Napoleon in the protracted war against France. Three years earlier in 1805 he had been in command of HMS *Defence* at the Battle of Trafalgar, when Nelson was shot and died aboard the *Victory*.

Sir George died when young James was only ten years old, but already he had imbued his young son with his own love of the sea. Eager to follow in his father's distinguished wake, James joined the Royal Navy when he was fifteen and by 1838 reached the rank of captain. While captain of HMS *Firebrand* he officially opened the River Parana in South America to navigation. Later during Britain's war with China he was appointed Commander in Chief in the Far East and his greatest success in this war over the opium trade, was the capture of Peking or Bejing as it is now known.

Admiral Hope was a popular leader with his ship's company and many men from Bo'ness requested specially to serve on board his ships. On one occasion one of these Bo'nessians saved the admiral's life. The sailor was Tom Grant from Carriden and the incident occurred during the China Campaign, when an enemy shell struck the deck and exploded almost at the admiral's feet. But for Grant's quick action in knocking him clear the admiral would have been killed by the explosion.

The fact that Admiral Hope had so many Scots in the crews aboard his ships probably accounts for his attempts to introduce special Scottish touches to the naval uniform, one of the main features of which was to have been a tartan Balmoral bonnet. This was actually introduced for a short time on an experimental basis, but it did not prove suitable because the wool retained too much moisture from the salt sea spray and Admiral Hope reluctantly abandoned the idea.

Although the Scottish uniform was not adopted, Hope did succeed in another of his bids to give life aboard ship a Scottish flavour. This he did by transforming the main deck of his man o' war into a makeshift theatre in which to stage Scottish plays. His favourite was Sir Walter Scott's *Rob Roy*, which provided plenty of action and fights for the sailors, who played the parts and for guests who were invited aboard in many ports to make up the audience for his floating repetory company.

Another of Admiral Hope's Scottish ideas was that like army regiments, naval vessels should bear Scottish names such as HMS *Carriden* and HMS *Kinneil* to encourage local recruitment from individual ports. He was also very conscious of the need to improve conditions on board from improving the diet to limiting the severity of floggings with the cat o' nine tails, so as to encourage voluntary enlistment instead of depending upon the hated press gang. Hope knew all about the work of the press gangs, because Bo'ness and Carriden with their many good sailors were amongst their favourite Scottish hunting grounds. Whenever a naval vessel was sighted out in the Forth it was said that local sailors used to hide in the woods behind Kinneil and Carriden or in the attics and cellars of the town's houses, especially it is said of those on Providence Brae, in case the dreaded press gang under

The tall spire of Carriden Parish Church is a landmark on the south shore of the Forth, midway between Bo'ness and Blackness. Its sailors' loft is on the north side, nearest the river, and in it can be seen the Rover, *a beautiful model sailing ship, which has been restored by Bo'ness sailing enthusiast, Mr Charles Sneddon, who also helped to organise the Tall Ships Race 1995 visit to the Forth.*

the cover of darkness rowed ashore with muffled oars, in an attempt to capture them and force them to serve in the navy.

By the time Admiral Hope died in 1881 he was happy to know that the need for impressment had disappeared and that the Royal Navy was well on course to become the modern force which was to serve Great Britain well in the two world wars of the next century. He was buried in Carriden Church yard, only a few metres from the spot on the Forth where his father had first taught him to sail, and his grave was surrounded by an anchor chain from one of the vessels he commanded.

Another naval grave in Bo'ness worth searching for is that of Captain Donald Potter. The captain was born in 1756, in the little village of Livingston, where the New Town now stands. While still a boy he joined the Royal Navy. During the Napoleonic War he took part in many sea battles while serving aboard several warships including, HMS *Bellona* and HMS *Princess*. It was, however, always the events of the Glorious First of June, 1794, when the British fleet under Admiral Howe routed the French navy, which he loved to recall, when he retired from active service and came to live with relatives in Bo'ness. With him he brought his war trophy, an old splintered cannon ball, which he had picked up after the battle and each year on the first day of June he delighted in decorating it with brightly coloured ribbons, then dressed in his full naval uniform and carrying the colourfully adorned souvenir of the battle, he began his celebrations by marching through the narrow streets of the town. He was always followed on his annual tours by a retinue of small boys, who waited outside every inn and pub, which the captain entered to toast his old admiral and the continued success of the British navy.

In 1830, Captain Potter had even more to celebrate because his many years of courageous and loyal service were marked by his appointment as a Commander in his Majesty's Forces (Retired). When he died, Captain Potter's cannon ball accompanied him on his last voyage to the old church yard on the Wynd and was placed above the crown and anchor carved on his gravestone.

From sailors to a famous soldier, Carriden was also the home of Colonel James Gardiner, who was born at Burnfoot in 1687 and who features in the writings of Sir Walter Scott as Edward Waverley's commanding officer. As a small boy Gardiner walked each day to attend Linlithgow Grammar School. As was the custom in the 17th century he enrolled as a cadet in the army while still very young and by the time he was fourteen obtained an ensign's commission in a Scots regiment in the Dutch service. In 1702 he obtained a similar commission in the British army from Queen Anne. At the Battle of Ramillies he was injured. While shouting to his men to urge them on a bullet entered his mouth. He thought at first he had swallowed it, but it had passed straight through his body and exited by a hole in the back of his neck. He collapsed on the field where he lay through the night until next morning he was found by the French who had come to plunder the dead. They were about to slaughter him with a sword, when one shouted, 'Don't kill that poor child' and he was instead carried to a nearby convent. There he was nursed by the nuns for several months and when recovered was held as a prisoner of war for a short time but was soon exchanged. Back in service he fought in several of the Duke of Marlborough's famous battles and rose to the rank of Colonel of the Dragoons. In 1745 he served with the government forces against the Jacobites and was one of those killed in the surprise dawn attack on Commander John Cope's troops at the Battle of Prestonpans. A plaque on the wall on the riverside path at Burnfoot describes him as, 'A brave soldier and a devout Christian' and bears a quotation from the Book of Timothy, Chapter Four, verse seven, which reads, 'I have fought a good fight, I have kept the faith'.

Today this site at Cuffabouts is the setting for the new sewage treatment works for the area, but for generations of Bo'ness children this was the seaside and in years before families jetted off to Spain and its Costas, going to the Crookies was a great summer holiday treat. Unlike most of the coast of the Forth there was actually a stretch of sand, well maybe shingle, at Crookies and many family picnics were held there. Why it was called the Crookies is a mystery. Perhaps at one time the family who sold bottles of lemonade from their solitary seashore home were called Crooks. It had certainly nothing to do with crooks, or robbers or crime, for the sale of lemonade was as far as commercialisation at this tiny holiday spot ever went and children could come alone and spend all day here in complete safety. On summer nights too the Crookies provided a romantic stroll and for the more energetic a chance to walk all the way down past the Fisheries where salmon were once netted and on to Blackness. At the end of the three mile hike there was always the promise of a wee refreshment in the inn, before turning round to walk the three miles home, which always seemed longer.

For several years the shore path from Carriden to Blackness was impassable without clambering into fields and over fences. Now it has been restored by a government youth opportunities scheme and is again one of the pleasantest walks along the whole length of the Forth with magnificent views across the river to the hills of Fife, while looking back upstream to the west the sunsets over Kincardine Bridge can often be spectacularly beautiful as the evening sky above Ben Ledi turns first a warm hot orange and then a glowing cinder red.

CHAPTER 13
BLACKNESS AND THE BINNS

While Bo'nessians of an evening may stroll, or nowadays more likely drive down to Blackness, Blackness has always been Linlithgow's territory. For it was as the official outport for the rival royal burgh and county town, that little Blackness grew and flourished from the 14th to the 17th centuries.

Like Bo'ness and Bridgeness further up river, Blackness does indeed stand on a 'nez' or nose of land jutting out into the Forth and the colour is indeed black, solid black basalt rock, which makes up the promontory on which its famous castle stands guard. Unlike Linlithgow's 'palace of pleasance' there is nothing pleasant about Blackness Castle. It is a grim guardian of a fortress, cold and forbidding.

Approach its outer yett with its heavy iron gate and it is immediately obvious how easily defended it was. Cunningly built at right angles to defeat the most vigorously wielded battering ram, its inner passageways offered the defenders every advantage and the enemy attackers none. The river provided Blackness with a natural moat and where the smooth green lawn today tempts visitors, in the past there was a treacherous salt marsh with only one secret path to offer safe passage.

Most intriguing aspect of the castle has always been its ship-shape design. Did it acquire this design simply because of its long narrow shape as the experts of Historic Scotland insist or was it really built like a medieval stone-hulled man o' war as local legend has always maintained? According to local tradition Blackness was built like a stone warship to fulfil a promise made by Archibald Douglas to James V, when the king made him Lord High Admiral of the Scottish Fleet. King Jamie was anxious for a flagship strong enough to defeat the English and Admiral Douglas promised him one which the 'auld enemy' could never sink. Blackness with its massive Stern Tower, its tall Main Mast Tower and its stone bows lapped by the waves of the river, is said to have been the result. Douglas is also said to have had an ulterior motive. Assuring his majesty that he was aboard ship at Blackness saved him from actually having to put to sea, where he knew he would be sea sick, every time!

In actual fact Blackness does not need any legends to lend it interest because its factual history is a sufficiently intriguing one. To begin with Blackness was a stronghold of the powerful Chrichton family, but in 1453 George Chrichton gave it as a gift to King James II and it has remained a property of the crown ever since. A captain or keeper of the castle was appointed and often this role fell to the Sheriff of Linlithgow, whose trade it guarded over.

From the outset the other role for Blackness Castle was as Scotland's version of France's grim Chateau d'If and as a state prison it held many captives of high rank. Most famous was Cardinal Beaton, who was held there for about four weeks in 1543.

That same year saw a great strengthening of the fortifications at Blackness, a task entrusted to Sir James Hamilton of Finnart, illegitimate son of the Earl of Arran. Finnart greatly increased its fire power and cannon were situated to give all round cover. The new defences were first put to the test only a few years later when Blackness remained loyal to Mary Queen of Scots from her abdication in 1567 until 1573 and even then it was never taken by an assault, but by a trick. In that year Mary's loyal supporter Sir James Kirkcaldy brought over from France one year's income from the Queen's French dowry. He could not deliver it to Edinburgh Castle as he had originally intended because it was being besieged by the supporters of Mary's son the young James VI and so he landed the money at Blackness, where he thought the governor was loyal. The governor, however, saw the funds as his opportunity to purchase his pardon from the Regent Morton and so took Kirkcaldy prisoner and rode off to Edinburgh with the cash. As soon as he was gone Kirkcaldy managed to persuade the French soldiers to revert to their original support for Mary. As soon as they freed him, he in turn, imprisoned the governor's brother who had been left in command.

When Regent Morton heard, he summoned the help of Kirkcaldy's wife to retake Blackness. Acting on the regent's instructions she rode out from Edinburgh and the delighted Kirkcaldy provided her with a lavish banquet in the great hall of the Stern Tower. The eating, drinking and merrymaking went on late into the evening, but Lady Kirkcaldy was strangely reluctant to spend

Blackness is often known as 'Scotland's ship-shape castle', and the reason can be clearly seen in this view taken from the Maid of the Forth *on one of her popular evening Three Bridge Cruises.* W F Hendrie.

the night. Instead she insisted that she must return to the capital and while accepting her husband could not safely enter the city, persuaded him that he should accompany her on the first part of the journey and bring most of the garrison to provide an escort.

Together they rode along the foreshore of the Forth, through the village square and up the steep hill behind it. All seemed well until they swung south at Mannerstoun to climb the next hill, when suddenly they were ambushed by the Regent's soldiers under the command of Captain Andrew Lambie. Kirkcaldy put up a brave fight but was overcome by Lambie's superior numbers. As Kirkcaldy cursed his ill fate, he was even more devastated to see his wife ride free and to realise she had been part of the plot and had betrayed him. In Edinburgh, Kirkcaldy was held prisoner in the castle, but managed to escape and sought his revenge. Soon afterwards Lady Kirkcaldy was found dead in her bedchamber. Her throat had been wrung. Later Lord Kirkcaldy was recaptured, charged with murdering his wife by strangling her, found guilty and executed.

During the reign of Mary Queen of Scots' son King James VI, Blackness was again used as a state prison, its captives including the Rev John Welsh, who was the son in law of John Knox. He was one of six Scottish ministers who were imprisoned by James VI because they insisted they had the right to meet in general assembly as a parliament of the kirk without the royal presence. Their defiance of the king's divine right enjoyed much support in Scotland and Lady Culross wrote assuring them that, 'the blackness of Blackness is not the blackness of darkness'.

Religious prisoners continued to fill Blackness well into the 17th century. The Abbot of New Abbey, William Brown was imprisoned in the tall Main Mast Tower, accused of being, 'a trafficking and seducing Papist'. Then in 1624 Edinburgh Bailie William Rigg was held captive for challenging the teachings of the Episcopalian Church, which James VI favoured. He was not alone however and soon many more Covenanting prisoners were confined in the dark, dank dungeons at Blackness. One of them was Adam Blackadder, the son of the Covenanters' leader, who described waking in the morning to find wee green puddocks and several big brown toads clambering all over him in his cell. This may have been the most horrible of the dungeons at Blackness, the terrible Black Pit. The Black Pit was situated right in the bows of the castle and at every high tide it was flooded with swirling salt river water, not to try to drown them as some of the soaking prisoners believed, but to provide a simple means of primitive sanitation, or so the castle authorities insisted.

Chief persecutor of the Covenanters was always alleged to be General Tam Dalyell, whose home, the Binns, overlooks Blackness and is according to local tradition directly linked to the castle prison by underground passage. Binns is a corruption of the Gaelic for hills and the Covenanters insisted that 'Bloody Tam' kept an array of instruments of torture in his hilltop hide-away including the dreaded thumb screws. They even maintained General Tam cooked Covenanters alive in the cavernous oven in the Binns kitchen and having dined off their roasted flesh, settled back to enjoy a game of cards with his favourite companion the Devil. Just pronounce his name, 'DL', they suggested and see with whom the General is in league!

One dark winter's night, however, Tam and Auld Nick apparently fell out over a hand at cards and the Devil, losing his temper hurled the gaming table out of the house. As a precaution against any further outbursts of demonic temper, Dalyell is said to have built the Binns turrets to pin his home down just in case the De'il tried to blow it away, but try as he might he never managed to retrieve his card table. Even after his death the table remained

Boats on the shore at Blackness. Ian Torrance.

missing for hundreds of years, until one day the soldiers of the regiment which he founded to hunt down the Covenanters, the famous Royal Scots Greys returned to the Binns. Watering their famous grey chargers at the pond beside the entrance drive, they suddenly noticed something sticking out above the surface. They harnessed their horses to the object and tugged and tugged until they pulled from the pond the long lost marble topped table. Now it is a prized exhibit in the laigh or lower entrance hall of the old house.

As far as General Tam was concerned founding the Scots Greys at the Binns in 1681 and cladding them in camouflage grey uniforms for which the cloth was specially imported from the Netherlands instead of the customary red coats of the period, was simply doing his job to the best of his ability and that job was to loyally serve his king. This was a royal allegiance he had already shown to the full over thirty years earlier when upon the execution of King Charles I by the Roundheads in 1649, he had sworn never to cut his hair or trim his beard until the monarchy was restored. As a sworn enemy of the new Lord High Protector Oliver Cromwell, General Tam went into exile at the start of the Republic and went instead to serve the Czar of Russia. He did an excellent job of reforming and modernising the Czar's army, but throughout his whole time in Russia never cut a hair of his head or from his beard, until in 1660, word reached him that King Charles II had been restored to the throne. To this day an oil portrait of the bearded general hangs in the Binns dining room and displayed along side it is the large bone comb he used to keep both beard and hair in order.

Once home, Dalyell immediately offered his services to the new monarch and as the royal bidding was to curb the Scottish religious rebels, the Covenanters, he did his utmost to obey. Amongst those he hunted down were many religious protesters from his own area including the Rev William Wishart of Kinneil Kirk. Mr Wishart steadfastly refused to adopt the Episcopalian prayers and order of service ordered by King Charles II and on 15th September 1660 was arrested by the authority of the Committee of Estates. He was imprisoned in the Tolbooth in the High Street in Edinburgh and went on to spend a year in captivity in Stirling Castle. On his release it was impossible for him to return to preach at Kinneil, but his congregation defied the Duke of Hamilton, who supported the King's Episcopalian views, by marching out of the church to listen to him at open-air services in the hills between Bo'ness and Linlithgow. At these hilltop services called conventicles, sentries were always posted to look out for Dalyell and his government soldiers. At the first sign of the troops, worship was abandoned and the communion vessels were even made collapsible so that the bowl of the communal cup could be hidden by one Covenanter, the stem by another and the base by a third. At first they generally managed to escape, but the coming of Dalyell's Royal Scots Greys made it ever more difficult and in the end the Rev Mr Wishart was captured again. This time he was sentenced on 25th February 1685 to be deported to the American colonies, a fate from which he was only saved by the death of his enemy King Charles II.

Despite the risks the Covenanters were not deterred. On one occasion Adam Blackadder wrote, 'They made my worthy old father climb dykes and hedges from one yard to another on a dark night till he got up the hill, where there was a barn in which he lay down all night. This was for being in Borrowstounness, where he had been preaching and baptised twenty-six children'.

Bo'ness was always a stronghold of the Covenanters often sheltering them until a favourable high tide or a 'Protestant tide' as it was often known, enabled them to escape by sailing away down river to seek the safety of Protestant Holland. Some Bo'nessians took their faith even further than others. One such was a tall ruggedly handsome sailor called Muckle Jock Gibb. Jock's beliefs were so strong he founded his own sect called the Sweet Singers of Borrowstounness. His followers who were mainly women took their name from the fact that they used to walk the streets of Bo'ness singing the most dolorous of Scottish psalm tunes. The Sweet Singers were also known as the 'Gibbites' after their leader, who they held in such high esteem that they called him 'King Solomon'. Amongst the edicts which he issued was a ban on using the names of the days of the week because they were derived from the titles of the pagan Scandinavian Gods such as Wodin, who gave his name to Wednesday and Thor, the God of War after whom Thursday was named. Muckle Jock also denounced both King Charles II and his government as most wicked and decreed his followers should not pay any taxes as they went to support king and parliament!

Most of his wrath was however directed against Edinburgh, whose inhabitants he considered to be completely depraved and living in a Scottish version of ancient Sodom. In the end he considered even the douce inhabitants of Bo'ness too wicked for his followers to live with and so on a freezing winter day early in 1681 he marched off with about thirty of his most devoted followers. Despite the pleas of their relatives and friends Muckle Jock and his supporters left the town and trekked on out into the Pentland Hills. Without food, water or suitable heavy clothing the Sweet Singers suffered greatly in the hills. Despite a plea from the Covenanting leader Donald Cargill, Muckle Jock refused to give in and return to Bo'ness, insisting that they were all going to stay in the Pentlands overlooking Edinburgh, until they saw the, 'smoke and utter ruin of the sinful and bloody city'.

By this time the presence of Gibb and his Sweet Singers was proving an embarrassment for the authorities in Edinburgh and a party of Dragoons were dispatched to Woodhill craigs to round them up. They were all marched into the city of their nightmares. Gibb and the men in the group were separated from the women and lodged in the Tolbooth prison in the High Street. Over twenty of the women were taken to the House of Correction, where they were stripped and whipped. After a short time they were all set free and went home to Bo'ness. This appears to have cured all of

The House of Binns, home of the Dalyell family since it was built in the 17th century. Forth Valley Tourist Authority.

the Sweet Singers apart from Muckle Jock himself. He continued his campaign against the Devil and was imprisoned again. When next heard of he was in America where he subsequently died, but whether he was transported there as a punishment or whether he went there voluntarily to escape the evils of everyday Scotland is not known. His life and adventures in the colonies did however provide the basis for John Buchanan's novel, *Salute to Adventurers*. His earlier escapades in the Pentland Hills also feature in another well-known piece of Scottish fiction, Crockett's, *Men of the Moss Hags*.

While Dalyell approved of the treatment of Jock and his followers, which he considered correct by the standards of his day, he was furious at the attack and massacre of Covenanters including women and children at Rullion Green, which was against his orders. From then on he refused to take any further part in the campaign against them and devoted himself to improving his estate at the Binns, including planting many trees. He also spent much time in his library, which was one of the largest in Scotland at that time and which a contemporary noted required a ladder to reach all the books. Despite these signs of a cultivated gentleman, the Covenanters never forgave him and even after his death insisted his ghostly apparition came back on his grey horse to haunt the house each night, riding endlessly from the Black Gates, which used to stand on the main Bo'ness to Queensferry road to the courtyard at the Binns and back again.

General Tam Dalyell. Forth Valley Tourist Authority.

The Binns must be one of Britain's most haunted mansions, because apart from the mounted figure of General Tam the house and its grounds are also said to be haunted by three other ghosts; the Devil, a small brown clad figure of a Pict, who is believed to have been one of the first inhabitants of the site and who is doomed forever to gather sticks; and a gleaming black horse-like water kelpie which lives in the same pond where the card table surfaced. In addition there is also the legend that like the apes on the Rock of Gibraltar ensuring that it continues to belong to Great Britain, so to does the presence of peacocks at the Binns guarantee that it will continue, as it always has done since the house was built, to be the home of the Dalyell family of whom the present occupiers are Tam, the well-known Labour MP for Linlithgow, his wife Kathleen, daughter of the late Lord Wheatley and their children Gordon and Moira.

In 1944 the Binns became the first private home gifted to the National Trust for Scotland, when it was entrusted to it by Tam's mother, Lady Eleanor Dalyell. Recently it has been reroofed and restored and has now been reopened to the public throughout the summer season, although it is still very much a lived in family home. As well as touring the house, including the royal bed-chamber with its elaborately decorated plaster ceiling which was prepared in 1633 for King Charles I, but never occupied, visitors can also follow the nature trail in the grounds, which leads up to the Binns Tower erected to mark the raising of the Royal Scots Greys.

When she handed over her home to the National Trust, Lady Dalyell retained two rights, to appoint the steward and to keep the long lost Binns treasure if it is ever unearthed, but like the tunnel from the house to Blackness Castle, it has never been discovered.

Lacking a tunnel the way back to the village overland leads past the small holdings, an agricultural experiment dating from the 1920s when small parcels of land were made available to try to bring to life the concept of a brave new world, as promised to the veterans of the First World War. The small holdings were however too small to be truly viable and today most are owned or tenanted by weekend farmers, who enjoy a taste of the good life but also have other week day jobs. There are some exceptions. One of the small holdings on the main Bo'ness to Queensferry road to the west of the entrance to the House of Binns and the cottages at Merilees, has expanded into one of Scotland's largest garden centres, complete with one of the country's first ostrich farms. Even more incongruous perhaps, is the name chosen for the centre by its Pakistani owners who have called it Rucken Glen, with all its west of Scotland connotations.

Back in the village another new name has appeared above the door of the old tearoom in the Square, which has become the Hamlet Cafe as a reminder of the exciting days during which Blackness was invaded by Australian film star Mel Gibson and the rest of the cast of Shakespeare's Danish tragedy, when Hollywood director Franco Zifferelli decided the castle would make an ideal setting for ghost of the king to appear on the battlements and other scenes from the famous play. Across the Square, Blackness Inn is still serving a cocktail called Hamlet on the Rocks, but is actually better known for its speciality catch of the day, excellent, succulent, mouth watering haddock supplied fresh daily by Linlithgow's

Todd the Fish Monger.

Since Blackness enjoyed the showbiz excitement of the filming of Hamlet, the castle has also been used for location shots for the historic drama, *The Bruce*, which also featured many local people as extras and the BBC television version of Sir Walter Scott's *Ivanhoe*. None of this can however approximate to the true excitement of the village's annual big day, the first Tuesday after the second Thursday in June, when as tradition demands it plays an important part in Linlithgow's annual Riding of the Marches. In the middle ages the three miles distance which separated the little port from the royal burgh, was considered too far for it to be governed by the provost and so Blackness was given its own official, the Baron Bailie. In medieval times he was a powerful figure with the right to fine and flog any sailors who became drunk or disorderly while in port. Today his main duty is to give his annual report on Marches Day after the provost's guests, the members of the Ancient Guild of Dyers and the other participants have all partaken of the potent whisky laced Blackness milk.

After the Baron Bailie's report all those riding the Marches climb up to the farthest flung outpost of Linlithgow's traditional territory, the ruins of St Ninian's Chapel on Castle Hill for the ceremony of the fencing of the court.

The other ceremony at Blackness on Marches Day is always the laying of a wreath at the war memorial in front of the village church with its unusual central spire. It was built during the First World War to provide a place of worship for the sailors of the Royal Navy ships moored out in the Forth. Originally an Episcopalian church, worship is now according to the rites of the Church of Scotland and Sunday services are conducted by the minister from Carriden Parish Church.

Inside the little church hangs a model sailing ship. Called *The Knowe* after the Bo'ness mansion where it was originally found it is a reminder of the days when Blackness was a port. Today, Blackness pier has been restored by the BBC, the Blackness Boat Club, but even now it is hard to picture the village as Scotland's second most important port as it once was. In the Square, however, the name of the block of unprepossessing council houses, the Guildry, is still a reminder of the large thick stone walled warehouse which previously occupied the shore-side site. There the members of the Linlithgow trade guilds stored their imports and exports.

In the 18th century Blackness gained what was for a time an important new trade, the export of tobacco to Holland, because as explained in earlier chapters the British Navigation Laws prevented its direct shipment from Virginia and the other colonies to the Netherlands. It was the tobacco trade which brought the village and Linlithgow their connection with the famous Mitchell family of Prize Crop fame. Local tradition has it that at one time the family planned to open the world's largest reference library in Linlithgow as a site central for the whole of Scotland, but in the end the now world famous Mitchell Library was built in Glasgow.

The Blackness story also contains other tales of missed opportunities. In Victorian times the village became a popular watering place for the families of Falkirk merchants and shop owners, rather in the way the Clyde holiday resorts benefited from Glasgow's patronage. Nosirrom and a few other houses were built along the shores of the east and west bays, but the big boom never came. Then fifty years later the proposal to make Blackness Bay Scotland's main passenger seaplane base was overtaken by the construction of land-based airports. Again following the Second World War, the time again seemed to have come for Blackness to expand when in 1947 holiday camp impresario Billy Butlin considered it for his Scottish development, but in the end decided to site it in the west at Heads of Ayr, where it still flourishes as Wonderwest. Whether little Blackness would have benefited or suffered from the involvement of Butlin is debatable, but the village now seems destined to remain a quiet backwater. Perhaps now the old pier at the castle, built originally to ship munitions without the danger of transporting them overland, has been redecked *The Maid of the Forth* or similar pleasure boats may bring a few extra tourists, but on the whole Blackness will continue to be the wee place local families drive down to on summer Saturdays and Sundays to simply sit and stare as the Forth flows by.

CHAPTER 14
HOPETOUN TO DALMENY

Making a much greater mark on Scottish tourism is nearby Hopetoun House, four miles further down river. Magnificent Hopetoun has always been owned by the Hope family, ever since it was first built in 1699 for the first earl.

Hopetoun is without doubt Scotland's finest stately home and in a way it offers its paying guests double the value for their money. For seen from the west, the original house designed by Sir William Bruce, who was also the architect of Her Majesty the Queen's official residence in Scotland, Holyrood Palace in Edinburgh, may still be viewed in all its 17th-century splendour overlooking its ornamental lake. Approached from the east, however, Hopetoun takes on an entirely different aspect and truly lives up to its description as Scotland's Versailles.

What happened was that in 1721 the Hopes decided they wanted to transform their still new home and after twenty years employed the country's leading architect William Adam to rebuild it in his grand Georgian style. Adam's design involved a strictly symmetrical design and to achieve this geometric precision, added two identical palace blocks to the north and south, which have the effect of framing the original building. At first sight the two blocks do conform exactly to Adam's strict rules of symmetry, but look closer and discover how this master craftsman utilised tromp d'oeil to achieve his desired effect with mock doors, windows and fanlights.

Behind the real or false doors too, the interiors of the two blocks are also entirely different, but their original uses were related. For while the southern palace today houses the beautiful tapestry-hung ballroom with its glittering candelabrum, it was originally an indoor riding school, where the family's horses practised the intricate haute ecole movements still shown on the 18th-century screens in the house's garden room, while the northern block contained the stables where they lived. In those days there was even an upstairs and downstairs regime among the Hopetoun horses, the spacious loose boxes enjoyed by the hunters can be contrasted with the stalls for the coach and farm horses as the stables and adjoining coach houses have been converted into the Scottish Museum of the Horse and will soon house the magnificent collection of horse drawn carriages, which formerly belonged to St Cuthberts Co-operative Society in Edinburgh.

Next door is an audio-visual display about the construction of Hopetoun and it is well worth visiting before climbing the steps to tour the house itself. The steps at Hopetoun's main entrance are the one aspect of the house, which do not appear to be exactly right and they are not. At either end they end in abrupt drops, but in the state dining room a large oil painting of the first earl shows him pouring over Adam's plans and the flight of steps are depicted as finishing with gracious curves. Did the Hopes change their minds about the design or did they grudge the extra expense or perhaps, rather than running short of cash they simply ran out of patience and wanted to see the work finished after so many years of construction turmoil?

Certainly the work took so long that it required William Adam's equally famous sons, John and Robert to complete the interior decoration, which was an integral part of all Adam's designs and which mirrored the external symmetry with similar use of tricks to achieve the exact geometric effect. At last in 1767 work on Hopetoun was eventually finished, but William Adam did not live long enough to see his Georgian masterpiece completed as he had died in 1748. One of Hopetoun's pleasant features is its sweeping vista views and from the entrance hall they can be admired stretching as far as the eye can see to east and west. An essential feature of these extensive vistas was that they must not be obstructed by walls, hedges or fences so that the herds of deer and flocks of sheep should appear free to roam right up to the house in a such of rural idyll. Again, however this was achieved by subtle trickery in the shape of cunningly hidden ditches called 'hahas', a name which reflects the great landscape artist, Capability Brown's appreciation of his own little joke.

Inside the house there are also many delightful touches from the wood-panelled main stairs, painted to reflect views of Hopetoun itself, to the Meissen ceramics displayed in several of the rooms. While the Adam green decorated entrance hall and the adjoining wood-panelled garden room, both at first seem large, they pale into insignificance compared with the scarlet and gold

The original west façade of Hopetoun House is seen in this view. Hopetoun is situated on the south shore of the Forth, midway between Blackness and Queensferry, and the river can be seen on the left. Forth Valley Tourist Authority.

decorated parade room. It takes its name from the fact that it was here guests were received before dinner and promenaded or paraded to and fro exchanging greetings and social chit chat. To allow for this all of the furniture was specially designed to line the walls, thus leaving the centre free of obstructions. The walls of the parade room are still lined with their original red silk. Look at the long wall mirrors and try to identify which of them are also originals.

Another of Hopetoun's spacious apartments with its original decoration is the splendid Yellow Drawing Room, which takes its name from the silk brocade adorning its walls. Look up and admire its plaster ceiling, which with its covered cornice, rococo spandrels and its gold frieze, decorated with animal masques, is one of the most ornate in Britain. Many of the Yellow Drawing Room's furnishings are also 18th-century originals, designed specially for Hopetoun by James Cullen, the Scottish carpenter, whose work rivals that of the English master craftsman, Thomas Chippendale. The drawing room also serves as the house's main art gallery and its treasures include Canaletto's, *The Grand Canal, Venice*, a huge hunting scene, which is believed to be a Titian and several Dutch

143

scenes by Backhuysen and Teniers. It would be particularly delightful to visit Hopetoun at Christmas as the Yellow Drawing room's most famous piece is Ruben's *Adoration of the Shepherds* and it would make the ideal setting for a carol concert, but unfortunately the house is closed from the beginning of October until Easter.

During its open season, however, Hopetoun's welcome is a particularly warm one thanks to its trust's policy of involving volunteer guides. Instead of being shown round, as in so many stately homes, Hopetoun encourages its visitors to take their time and linger as they please. Instead of groups being shown round therefore, visitors make their own way and are welcomed in each room by one of the volunteers who are always ready to talk, explain and answer questions. Among the rooms which also elicit most queries are the ornate Bruce Bedchamber with its four-poster complete with overhead tester and rich drapes, the book lined library and billiard room and the dining room whose long table is set for dinner.

In the dining room, the gleaming brass plant stands are decorated with elephant heads, a reminder that India was among the countries of the British Empire in which the Hopes held distinguished posts as Viceroys and later Governors General and the museum at Hopetoun contains many other souvenirs of their service abroad. Amongst them is the emu, which was brought home from Australia and lived happily for many years in Hopetoun's eight hundred acres of parkland until it died of old age and was stuffed and put on display. Less politically correct are the ferocious tiger heads, which snarl down from the walls of the entrance to the house's restaurant, as a reminder of the days, when it was considered sport to shoot India's wildlife.

Today's sports at Hopetoun are much less violent, with the grounds used for equestrian eventing and the lawns laid out for croquet. Hopetoun also has a garden centre and employs its own countryside rangers, who have laid out nature trails, which offer many views of the river below. For the most impressive panoramas of the Forth, however, it is well worth climbing the flights of stairs up to the rooftop viewing platform. From there it is possible to look both across the river to Fife and all the activity at Rosyth and downstream to the two Forth Bridges.

From Hopetoun the main drive leads down to the shores of

the river and just to the west of the suitably elaborate gates on the shores of the Forth lies the little hamlet of Society. How it got its name is a mystery. It was here that the Hopes came down to take the waters, so perhaps they were referred to as 'high society'. Small sailing vessels also berthed at Society to bring coal for the big house, so possibly these loads were described as being delivered to 'the society folk'. On their outward voyages the little sailing ships sometimes carried cargoes of limestone from the Hopetoun Estate. Sadly the old inn, where the sailors refreshed themselves between voyages has long closed, but picnics at this sandy cove are still a popular summer attraction.

The road from Society hugs the coast past quaint old Fisheries Cottage, before leading through a disappointing modern housing scheme into Queensferry, but at this point it is worth making a detour to visit some of the other villages around the Hopetoun Estate.

Most historic is undoubtedly tiny Abercorn, because it is mentioned several times in his writings by the Venerable Bede. According to this early churchman, when Aegfrid, King of Northumbria, whose kingdom included Lothian, was killed in battle by the Picts, Bishop Trumuini, in whose diocese it lay, considered Abercorn to be exposed to Pictish raids from across the Forth in Fife and therefore ordered the evacuation of the monastery of Aebercurnig, until peace returned.

In the 13th century Abercorn belonged to John Graeme, who supported Sir William Wallace and who fought and died at the Battle of Falkirk in 1298. The estate then passed into the possession of the Black Douglases and suffered when they challenged the Stewarts for the Scottish throne. Abercorn Castle, which was a simply square thick stone-walled peel tower or keep was their home until King James II beseiged it during the early months of 1455. After several attacks, the Douglas stronghold was finally stormed and captured on 8th April. The Douglases and their supporters were all killed and Abercorn Castle was destroyed.

The victorious Stewarts gave Abercorn to the third son of the Earl of Arran, Claud Hamilton, first Viscount Paisley. During the 16th century the Hamiltons forfeited Abercorn because they remained loyal to Mary Queen of Scots, but later the lands were restored to them by her son King James VI, who in 1606 created the first Earl of Abercorn. After that Abercorn changed hands several times in quick succession from the Hamiltons to the Mures and then to the Lindsays and the Setons and finally Sir Walter Seton sold it in 1678 to a prosperous Edinburgh butter merchant, John Hope. His son became the first Earl of Hopetoun and the Hopes, with their motto 'Hope, never broken', have retained it ever since.

Meanwhile although the monastery at Abercorn had died out it continued as one of Scotland's earliest parish churches, parts of which date from Norman times in the 11th century. Most of the church was, however, built after the Reformation in the 16th century and it was renovated at the start of Queen Victoria's reign in 1838. At this time it was floored for the first time and its walls were plastered. An early form of coal-fired central heating was also installed.

Writing in the Second Statistical Account of Scotland in 1843, Abercorn's minister, the Rev Lewis Irving, describes it as, 'a comfortable place of worship, nearly adequate to the wants of the community. There are no sittings let, the whole, with the exception of the private seats of the heritors, being allotted to the parishioners'. Today among the most interesting features of Abercorn are the private aisles belonging to the Hope family and to the Dalyells of the Binns. The latter contains the stones dedicated to the memory of the parents of Linlithgow's Member of Parliament, Tam Dalyell. The Hope Aisle overlooks the pulpit and its ornately carved wooden facade has been restored and painted by well-known Scottish architect and artist, Hubert Fenwick. Abercorn's church bell is also of interest having been originally the ship's bell of one of the Danish vessel's captured by the British navy under Admiral Lord Nelson at the Battle of Copenhagen during the Napoleonic War. The extensive immaculately kept graveyard, which surrounds the kirk, is worth browsing through as many of the stones are carved with symbols of the jobs which those who lie buried beneath used to do on the Hopetoun Estate. The tradition of naming workers' children after members of the Hope family can also be detected on several of the stones.

Climb over the little stone style and notice the historic postbox set in the wall. The big house which dominates the whole of this little hamlet was formerly the church manse. It looks enormous, bigger indeed than the little kirk which it overlooks and is perhaps a reminder of the former power of the church in the days during Victorian times when the minister could record that out of a congregation of 390 the average attendance at communion was no less than 350! Today Abercorn is reduced to sharing a minister with Dalmeny Kirk.

A church roll of almost four hundred is a reminder of just how many people were formerly employed on Hopetoun Estate and how modern methods of farming have reduced the population here as in other parts of rural Scotland, while the custom of having much smaller families has shrunk it still further. One place that still offers some local employment is the Hopetoun Sawmill on the road west out of the hamlet, before it sweeps up the hill to Whitequarries, between fields alive with pheasants.

Whitequarries is the site of Abercorn Primary School, a distinctly Victorian building completed in 1878. Before then the children of the Hopetoun Estate workers were educated in a single classroom in the hamlet of Abercorn, but although it was a one teacher school, it had one of Scotland's most famous dominies. Christopher Dawson was a teacher well before his time, believing in taking his pupils out of the classroom for nature walks through the Hopetoun Woods and for swimming expeditions to the shore at Society. On these outings all of the pupils were encouraged to gather items, which interested them and take them back for display in the classroom. The little Abercorn school collection, became so famous that it was often visited by distinguished visitors to Hopetoun House and they in turn were encouraged on their next visits to bring back exotic items from all over the world.

Parents were at first sceptical about the new 'maister', but when the parish minister and the elders of the Abercorn Kirk Session came to the school to conduct their annual inspection, they expressed themselves entirely satisfied with the standards which they found. One reason may have been the strict discipline, which the new dominie at first imposed with the lithe leather tawse, which he brought with him from his first school across the Forth in Cupar, in Fife. 'Be careful to check the smallest acts of disobedience and you will never be troubled with any great ones', he wrote and proved he meant it by wielding his supple strap as effectively as he did the fishing rod with which he passed his leisure hours on the estate. When, however, his pupils were suitably convinced that his strap stung as effectively as any snake, he decided he could dispense with corporal punishment, which he did in as public a fashion as he had administered his beltings.

His biographer, Jean Butler, who was his niece, described what happened as follows. 'One day in school an interesting and amusing ceremony took place. The faithful tawse, which had proved such a useful ally during the first few months, were declared to have served their purpose and outlived their usefulness and were solemnly cut in pieces, some of the girls carrying away the bits as trophies of a bygone age.'

Dominie Dawson's liberty to teach in his own fashion was threatened in 1874, when the government decided to impose standards on all Scottish schools and issued a curriculum and laid down methods, which its faceless civil servants in the Scottish Office in far off Dover House in London, decreed must be obeyed in every detail. Dawson was not afraid to put pen to paper and wrote, 'It is now expected that children shall be regularly turned out by the gross, like so many little human vessels duly warranted to contain a certain amount of human knowledge'. Unlike many of the other old style dominies, who gladly accepted the offers of pensions, however, Dawson persevered with the new order and despite complaining that he had been reduced, 'to nothing more than a grant earning machine', set about bringing his own distinctive flair to the new curriculum. Every morning he opened the school an hour early in order to have enough time to teach his own ideas, without endangering his pupils' chances in the official tests. His methods paid off, because in the first of the new style inspections, carried out by one of the first of Her Majesty's Inspectors, instead of the minister and his session, he was awarded, 'the highest possible grant for discipline and organisation'.

Soon afterwards Dawson and his scholars were also rewarded by the building of the new grey Gothic stone school building at Whitequarries on the main Bo'ness to Queensferry Road, but just when they might have enjoyed their spacious new premises, the roll was suddenly swollen by an unexpected invasion of new pupils. They were the children of the miners, who flocked to live in the area, when it was discovered that the West Lothian shale measures extended further to the north east than had been previously supposed and a mine was sunk next to the school. The area's shale oil boom had begun and soon long lines of miners' rows were constructed at Woodend and what became known as The Newton was built. Other mines were sunk still further east in Dalmeny and the workings stretched right out under the Forth as the miners followed the shale measures, which cropped up again on a limited scale across the Forth in Fife.

Working the shale seams was as drouthy work as any other form of mining and so it was not surprising that The Newton soon acquired its own pub, the Duddingston Arms, which is still a popular local hostelry with both a public bar and a snug little lounge. The Newton also acquired its own whitewashed village store and it claims to be the first petrol filling station in Scotland as it was through it that the Marquess of Linlithgow obtained the fuel he needed for his car, which was the first in the whole district. At first the petrol was transported once a week from Leith Docks in one gallon metal cans brought to the village store by horse drawn cart. Soon however the Marquess persuaded the grocer to invest in one of the newfangled petrol pumps. The handcranked pump was duly installed next to the general store and to this day the site is occupied by one of the busiest filling stations in the area.

From The Newton, the road swings on along the crest of the hill above the river and the lay-by on the left-hand side provides one of the best places to stop to view and photograph both Rosyth on the far shore and the two Forth Bridges. On the other side across the fields can be caught glimpses of Dundas Castle. For long known locally as the 'Secret Castle', because it was very strictly a private home, Dundas is now being opened up as a centre for small conferences and wedding receptions, thanks to the enterprise of its owner Sir Jack Stewart-Clark, European Member of Parliament for East Sussex who recently inherited the property. Dundas is everything a castle should be with solid stone walls, a tower and castellated battlements. This ancient baronial fortalice dates back to the eleventh century and the peaceful Norman Conquest of Scotland. It was strengthened in 1416 by warrant of Robert Duke of Albany and King James I agreed to its further fortification eight years later in 1424. Its walls reach a height of seventy five feet and as it stands over three hundred and fifty feet above sea level the views from its turrets out over the river and the bridges is breathtaking. Now visitors will have the chance to appreciate these views as dawn breaks, because Sir Jack has decided to welcome guests to his family home in what will be one of Britain's most up market bed and breakfast operations.

Long before Dundas was home to the Stewart-Clarks, it was however, headquarters of the Dundas family who occupied it for over seven hundred and fifty years. They obtained a charter to these lands from King David I. Twelve generations later James de Dundas gave a piece of his land down on the shore of the Forth, 'lying in the toun of the Ferry, for the church of St Mary the Virgin and for the construction of certain buildings to be erected there in the form of a monastery'. The good Sir James also gave the money to build both church and monastery on condition that prayers be said for, 'the souls of the grantor and his wife and ancestors and successors', and it is good to know that his wish is still faithfully complied with twice a year at the Patronal Festival on 16th July and again on 1st November, which is, of course, All Souls' Day. For although only a few of the foundations of the monastery, which became a house of the Carmelite Order survive, the church, with its unusual stone flagged roof, still stands in Queensferry High Street and is the place of worship of the burgh's Scottish Episcopalian congregation.

Unfortunately St Mary's benefactor, Dundas, died without a male heir and in 1450 was succeeded by his brother, Sir Archibald. His son and successor played an influential role at the Scottish royal court and King James III appointed him as ambassador in London. In 1488, James rewarded him for his services at the English court by creating him Earl of Forth, but very unfortunately for Dundas, the king died before placing his royal seal on the warrant of approval and it was deemed invalid.

Despite this set back the Dundas family continued to prosper. At the time of the Reformation in 1560, the last Roman Catholic Prior at St Mary's, Father Thomas Young, handed back the buildings and land to the Laird of Dundas and this deed was later confirmed by Mary Queen of Scots by a charter dated 5th April, 1564. During the 17th century St Mary's was at first still used by the townsfolk as their place of worship, but in 1635 they moved along the High Street to the then new parish church, whose plain unadorned interior and exterior must have seemed to make it a much more suitable setting for their Protestant services.

The Dundas family, however, still continued to use St Mary's as their burial place and the church still contains several of their memorials. They include a carved coat-of-arms on the east wall and a tombstone slab, dated 1608, in what is now the baptistry, where the font is also dedicated to the memory of several members of the family, as are several of the stained-glass windows, which

Victorian Dundas Castle, with the medieval keep in the background.

were installed in 1889, when St Mary's was restored mainly through the efforts of Bishop Dowden of Edinburgh. Sadly by then all of the domestic buildings of the monastery, its cloisters and the nave of the church had all been demolished, their stones perhaps utilised in the building of houses along the High Street, but architect James Kinross did a fine job of preserving and utilising what remained. This consisted of the chancel, with its lofty high pitched vault, the rectangular tower and the south transept. The transept was originally a side chapel and it now houses the baptistry, whose beautiful font with its panels depicting Matthew, Mark, Luke and John and its cover decorated with a carved angel, were all designed by the famous architect Sir Robert Lorimer of Kelly Castle in Fife.

Another interesting feature of the present church links it directly with the period when the Dundas family gifted this delightful place of worship to the town. This is the little guard window, which looks down from the inside of the tower into the chancel. It was from up there that one of the Carmelite brothers could keep watch to make sure no-one dared steal the sacred gold communion cups from their little stone cupboard to the left of the altar, or perhaps just slip in to enjoy an illicit sip of the communion wine. Other relics of these early days, which can still be found by the modern history detective include the stone sedilia or clergy seats so that they could rest during the lengthy services and on the right-hand side of the sanctuary, the piscina or sink, where the communion vessels were carefully rinsed after mass.

Today its Dundas benefactors would no doubt be delighted with the way in which St Mary's is furnished and obviously cherished by the members of its congregation. Their modern

151

additions well complement its ancient treasures and are also worth looking at. In a way the oil painting, *Scapular Vision* links the two. Painted by Donald Gorrie, it hangs to the left of the chancel arch and depicts the most important happening in the history of the Carmelite Order. This took place after the failure of the Crusades in the Holy Land obliged the Friars to abandon their Church of the Blessed Virgin on Mount Carmel and to wander throughout Europe. Each place they settled they founded another church to St Mary of the Mount. Throughout this difficult period their Prior-General, St Simon Stock, prayed for a sign that his Carmelite Order would survive and on 16th July, 1251, his prayers were answered, when the Holy Mother appeared before him in a vision and touching his scapular, from which the painting takes its title and which was his shoulder cape, promised that the order would have her special protection. Although this happening took place in England, the picture of it in St Mary's includes many local touches, including St Margaret landing from a ferryboat and the distinctive tower of the church overlooking the Forth.

The close connection St Mary's has always had with the river since the days when the monks gave shelter to the pilgrims waiting to cross on the ferry to the present day are also recalled by several items. These include the ensign and crest of HMS *Temeraire*, a naval training establishment, whose young members worshipped in the church until the school moved south to Dartmouth in 1960. It was on that occasion they presented these mementoes to St Mary's and they are now displayed at the foot of the tower. Outside facing the river, in the middle of the monastery garden or garth, is situated a large anchor and it well symbolises the place this unusual church has filled in the history of Queensferry. Outside also on the right-hand side of the most easterly of the windows on the High Street side is a very interesting sundial. It is a mass dial and was used to fix the times of the services in the centuries before the invention of clocks.

Time too to leave the church the Dundases financed and move back to the family themselves. From the time James Dundas was denied his earldom in 1488, they passed through another twelve generations before they faced another crisis in 1792, when the family line seemed doomed because the laird died without an heir. As captain of the East India Company's merchant vessel *Winterton* he was navigating his ship off the coast of Madagascar, when she hit a reef and he was drowned. Fortunately however, this tragedy had a happy ending, because six months later in January 1793, his wife gave birth to a healthy baby boy.

The baby was given the favourite family name of James and when he grew up it was he who decided to replace the original castle keep with a fine new grey stone Victorian mansion, but one which was still suitably adorned with towers and turrets in truly Scottish baronial style. The extra accommodation, which it provided did in indeed come in useful, because his wife, Lady Mary, daughter of the famous British national hero Admiral Lord Duncan, who won the great sea battle against the Dutch at Camperdown in 1797, presented him with eleven children, six boys and five girls.

Six years before his death in 1881, Sir James sold Dundas to James Russell Esq, from whom it passed to the Stewart-Clark family. The estate is at its colourful best in early summer, when the rhododendrons bloom and it is occasionally opened to the public in aid of charity.

Half a mile further to the east lies the Echline, which is said to have taken its unusual name from Queen Margaret's brother, Prince Edgar Ethling. The old stone-built Echline farm house still stands, but most of its fields are now covered with undistinguished modern homes.

Surprisingly, Dalmeny, another mile to the east, has not been swamped with new housing to the same extent and still retains its village charm. Set on either side of its spacious village green, Dalmeny has a decidedly English feel to it and this is added to by the square Norman tower of the village's famous little church. The tower, is however, the one aspect of Dalmeny Kirk, which is not genuine, because it was added during the renovations carried out in 1926 and is felt by many people to be somewhat overwhelming and out of proportion. Otherwise the church is without doubt the finest example of Norman architecture in Scotland. Dalmeny dates from the middle of the 12th century and may well have been built by the same masons who built Durham Cathedral, as much of its stonework bears the marks of their craftsmanship and like Durham it is dedicated to the great east coast saint, St Cuthbert.

The church is eighty four feet long and twenty five feet wide at its broadest part. Built facing east, as custom demanded so that worshippers might kneel in prayer facing towards Jerusalem, it consists of a small semi-circular apse, a square chancel and a rectangular nave, intended for the people of the village to use as their parish church. Both the roughly hewn arches between the apse and chancel and the chancel and the nave are carved with the typically Norman chevron zig-zag design. The eight corbels in the apse and chancel all bear grotesque carved faces of men and beasts. Beside the outer corbels of the apse, the holes in the wall were made to support a screen so that on special holy occasions, such as during Lent, the inner sanctuary could be divided from the rest of the church.

Originally all of the windows in the church were of plain glass, but at the end of the Second World War the officers of the Free Polish Army, who had been stationed in the area, gave the beautiful stained-glass windows, which now adorn the apse. The central lancet window depicts the Madonna and infant Jesus, pictured beside a proud Polish eagle, while the two small windows on either side show St Margaret with all her local connections and St Theresa, who like the eagle has special significance for the soldiers' homeland.

Dalmeny's other principle adornment lies outside, above the south door, which was originally the main entrance to the church. Here the fascinating double carved arch is home to a whole menagerie of real and legendary animals. The heraldic beasts include a dragon, phoenix, griffin, centaur, serpent and sea monster, while the real animals range from a lion to a lamb and from a pelican to a whale. One of the stones may also depict wild men, or savages, fighting. Why they were all painstakingly carved is an unsolved mystery. Perhaps they were a test for the young apprentice masons. For centuries they were shielded by a porch, the marks of which can be seen on the adjacent walls, below the four stone columns, but now they are without shelter and sadly exposed to the weathering effects of wind and rain.

Back inside the church other features particularly worth noting are the unusual carved wooden pulpit with its miserere or prayer stool, which is rarely found in a Scottish kirk and the much more typically Scottish, laird's loft. The idea of the laird's loft was that it was entered separately from the main body of the kirk, so that the laird and his family, in this case the Roseberys from Dalmeny House, need not pass through the rest of the congregation on the way to their pews.

Many of the neat little rows of grey stone cottages in Dalmeny housed the workers and their families from Lord Rosebery's farms at Easter and Wester Dalmeny. Towering over them were the solidly built manse, the minister's home, to the north of the church and to the east of it the headmaster's school house. It is good to know that after the day's lessons were over and the four o'clock bell had rung, the dominie always enjoyed the privilege of playing a round of golf on his lordship's private course within the grounds of Dalmeny House. The old school still stands in the centre of the village, overlooking the little war memorial, but it has now been converted into a community centre, while the children attend classes in its modern equivalent on the outskirts, overlooking the dual carriageway to Edinburgh. For a time its roll was boosted by the attendance of the sons and daughters of servicemen from the army's Scottish Headquarters, Craigiehall, but in line with military cut backs their numbers have dropped. Dalmeny's main source of employment, the Royal Alexandra Naval Victualling Yard also suffered a similar decline. The village does however still have its little general store, its post office and its joiner's shop, but the smiddy where the farrier once shod so many horses, has closed.

From the village the road east leads to Dalmeny Estate behind its high stone walls on the far side of the old main road from Queensferry to Edinburgh, each entrance guarded by a neat little stone built gatehouse. Now, however, the gates have been thrown open and visitors are welcome at Dalmeny House or Dalmeny Park, as it was originally known, throughout the whole summer season from May to September, when it is open each afternoon from Sunday to Thursday.

Dalmeny has belonged to the Earls of Rosebery's Primrose family for over three hundred years and today it is the home of the seventh Earl and Countess. The present house overlooking the river was designed at the end of the Napoleonic Wars, in 1815, by William Wilkins and appropriately it contains the fifth Earl's fascinating Napoleonic collection. The Napoleon Room is hung with paintings of the French Emperor and is furnished with the splendid pieces which he used at the height of his power. In stark contrast is the plain little desk and chairs from Longwood, his prison home on the island of St Helena, where he spent his final days in lonely isolated exile. Most ironically the collection also includes the campaign chair used by the Duke of Wellington throughout the long hard fought Peninsula Campaign in Spain and

Dalmeny House, home of the Rosebery family.

Portugal and when he finally defeated Napoleon at the Battle of Waterloo.

Dalmeny's main claim to fame, however, is as home to the Rothschild Collection of superb French 18th-century furniture, tapestries and porcelain, which was brought north from the Rosebery's English family home at Mentmore in Buckinghamshire. The collection came into the Rosebery family's possession through the marriage in 1878 of Archibald fifth Earl of Rosebery, who later became Liberal Prime Minister, to Hannah, only daughter of Baron Meyer de Rothschild. The priceless collection of items at Dalmeny were all chosen by the present Earl, before the famous sale at Mentmore in 1977.

Dalmeny House is a veritable art gallery, the collection including many 18th-century portraits by Gainsborough, Lawrence, Raeburn and Reynolds as well as tapestries by Goya. Of particular interest is the grand painting of the third Earl and his wife and family, pictured in the grounds at Dalmeny by Alexander Naismith.

Dalmeny was the first Tudor Gothic Revival house to be built in Scotland and architectural highlights include the Coade stone exterior decoration and the Gothic splendour of the hammer-beamed hall and the fan vaulted corridors. There is an exhibition showing how Wilkin's design for the house came to be chosen from a range of proposed designs submitted by Robert Adam and other leading architects.

Much more intimate and human than the other rooms at Dalmeny is the former prime minister Lord Rosebery's study, which has been left just as though he may return at any moment. Here it was that he received Gladstone at the start of the famous Mid-lothian Campaign, but the room also represents his own personal interests, especially his passion for horse racing and his colours are on display. They were borne by no fewer then seven Derby winners from his Mentmore Stud and a statue of one of his favourite horses, King Tom, stands outside the front door.

No visit to Dalmeny House is complete without exploring the grounds of its extensive parkland from the enclosed garden to the sheltered walk through the azaleas, rhododendrons and trees brought home by members of the family from all parts of the world and planted here. The walk leads to the Garden Valley. Highlight of any tour of the grounds however has to be the four and a half mile long coastal path, which leads all the way from Queensferry to Cramond and which offers amongst the best views to be had of the Forth. It also affords wonderful views of Barnbougle Castle in whose library Prime Minister Rosebery sought peace and quiet to write his speeches. The shore walk is open all year, free of charge and every day except Fridays there is a passenger ferry across the River Almond at the Cramond end, which plies on request and on payment of a small fee until 7 pm on summer evenings and until 4 pm on winter afternoons. The path runs through interestingly varied scenery from sheltered woodlands to open paths and passes both mud flats and sandy beaches, where many varieties of sea birds may be seen. The birdlife is often particularly plentiful in winter when North Sea gales or on calm days the gray clinging haars for which the Forth is so famous, lead many species to seek shelter on Dalmeny's shores.

Another special reason for visiting Dalmeny out of season is for the special February Sunday charity opening of Mons Hill, when its white carpet of snow drops is a promise that spring is only weeks away. Visitors to Dalmeny Estate should note that dogs are not allowed and that they are not permitted to build fires or picnic, but on days when the house is open to visitors this last restriction is well compensated for by the home baking in the restaurant in its now covered and converted courtyard.

CHAPTER 15
VALLEYFIELD TO LIMEKILNS

Across on the north shore we stopped at Culross and before moving on through Fife, its Abbey provides a fine lookout point from which to survey the river. From a quarter of a mile in width at Kincardine the Forth has now expanded to an impressive three miles. Some of that breadth is however being gradually reduced by the reclamation of Culross Bay by dumping the red ash waste from Longannet Power Station from where it is conveyed by rail along the shore of the river. One sad aspect is that the reclamation will eventually engulf little Preston Island, whose ruined buildings often intrigue motorists driving along the coast road through Low Valleyfield. These are not remains of a castle or a monastery as some imagine, but of an ambitious industrial project. It was the brainchild of Sir Robert Preston, who led the search for the heart in Culross Abbey and in a way the work on Preston Island, which was named after him, was typical of the same questing spirit.

Preston was brought up at Valleyfield House and like most boys brought up beside a river, soon learned how to handle a boat. His favourite voyage was out to the island, which was part of his family's estate. His boyhood boating expeditions gave him such a love for the sea, that when he grew up he made it his career. He joined the East India Company and eventually rose to captain one of their famous merchantmen, carrying rich cargoes of cinnamon, nutmeg and other spices along with equally expensive and luxurious fine silks home from the company's trading posts in the East Indies and India.

On leave in London, Sir Robert, as he had become, was a guest at many of the parties and balls given by the capital's high society and it was at one of them that he met and fell in love with the daughter of a prosperous merchant. On his succession to the family estate in Fife, Sir Robert brought his young wife to stay at Low Valleyfield. With his knowledge of trade and his contacts in London, he at once began to develop the estate and it was while searching for ways to do so he remembered his childhood voyages out to Preston Island. While playing on it he had often stumbled over small outcrops of coal and now as he hunted for some means to improve his finances, he remembered Sir George Bruce's 17th-century Moat Pit just a little further up the coast in Culross Bay.

Now with a site on the island for a much better shaft than was possible out in the river and with steam pumps to cope with any inrushes of water, Sir Robert decided to repeat the experiment on Preston Island. The huge advantage he saw for his island pit was again that in those days, when road transport of heavy loads was still practically impossible, ships could carry cargoes of coal direct from a berth immediately adjacent to the top of the shaft on the shore of the island, to London and other markets on the continent.

Like Sir George Bruce before him, Sir Robert Preston did not believe in any waste and so the dross not fit for export was used to feed the fires beneath the salt pans, which he soon established. Salt production on Preston Island proved so successful that a cluster of pans was soon busily at work on the shore and the red glow from their fires, burning both by day and by night, became a well-known beacon for sailors on the Forth.

Salt production on Preston Island might have continued as a profitable exercise for many years, had the coal pit which supplied its fuel not come to as violent an end as the Moat Pit, which was flooded by the mad March gale, which swept the whole of Scotland on the same night in 1625 that King James VI died in London. In the case of Preston Island Pit, however, it was not flood but fire, which led to its destruction. Shortly after the Preston miners, working over eight metres down, reached the rich coals of the Lochgelly Splint, there was an explosion caused by fire damp, methane gas. The blast and the flames which subsequently raged through the underground workings killed all of the miners. The explosion also ripped the roof off one of the passageways and allowed the river to break through, thus drowning Sir Robert's enterprising scheme.

That was not, however, the end of Preston Island's industrial story. The colliery buildings were soon taken over unofficially by a much more romantic business, the distilling of illicit whisky. The island made a first rate hide-away for such an illegal activity. It was ideally suited for smuggling the moonshine away down river. Rumours however soon began to spread about the Forth's island distillery and they reached the ears of the excise men based at the

Dinghies sailing on the Forth.

port of Bo'ness on the opposite shore. They waited for the first moonless night and just as the island stills were at their most productive staged a raid. All of the equipment was confiscated and production came to an abrupt end.

A century and a half later Low Valleyfield again became the centre for another daring Forth enterprise, when its colliery became the Fife end of the 'Funnel', as the miners quickly nick-named the Forth Tunnel. The tunnel, which reached a depth of four hundred and twenty metres beneath the bed of the Forth ran right under the river from Low Valleyfield to Kinneil on the south shore. The tunnel was in total just under three and a half miles long, the extra distance compared to the actual width of the river being accounted for by the fact that the underground workings at Low Valleyfield and Kinneil which it connected did not run in a straight line.

A much greater difficulty for the engineers who planned the 'Funnel' was the considerable difference in level of the two sets of workings. On the Fife side the workings were mainly four hundred metres deep. At Kinneil they were much deeper, some as far down as six hundred metres. The problems were solved however and on 30th April, 1964 mine driver Martin 'Tiger' Shaw broke through the last remaining centimetres of sandstone. The manager of Kinneil Colliery, David Archibald, stretched his hand through the gap to shake hands with his opposite number at Low Valleyfield, Norman Wallace and told him, 'I hope you've plenty of coal for me!', because it had been decided that all of the output

Forth Bridge and Ferry, South Queensferry.

should be processed at Kinneil as it had much more modern equipment including the newest washing plant in the country.

The coal was transported right under the river by incline planes and then by a narrow gauge electric railway and for almost twenty years helped to maintain Kinneil as a viable colliery, when geological difficulties made it difficult to work its own seams. In the end however competition from foreign cheap coal imports made the operation of the 'Funnel' uneconomical and although they were still rich seams left untapped, first Low Valleyfield Colliery and then Kinneil Pit were both closed.

Apart from the 'Funnel' the Victorian dream of crossing the Forth by tunnel as an alternative to a bridge was never realised. A century later another equally ambitious 1930s scheme to provide a crossing of the Forth by constructing a giant barrage dam was also unsuccessful.

The plan was put forward by two Bo'ness businessmen, architect Mathew Steele and hotelier John Jeffrey. Together they travelled the Forth valley towing a scale model of the proposed barrage on a trailer behind their car and addressed dozens of public meetings in village and town halls on both sides of the Forth.

At the time the two enthusiasts were mocked for putting forward an impractical plan, but now that similar barrage plans are being considered for the Solway and Severn and one was even drawn up for the English Channel perhaps they were simply far too far ahead of their time and their ideas are worth re-examining.

In the depressed early years of the 1930s the first advantage which Jeffrey and Steele claimed for their dam was that constructing it would create far more jobs locally than building a road bridge. Whereas building a suspension bridge would have required skilled steel erectors and spidermen to be brought in from other parts of the country the barrage dam would have required millions of tons of whin stone which could have been dug by the many unemployed West Lothian miners. More unskilled labourers could have been employed demolishing the local coal and shale bings whose spent blaes would have been needed as infill. Once built, as well as providing a four lane highway, cycle paths and footpaths along the top of it the barrage would also have created a hydro electric scheme providing cheap power for local industries in both West Lothian and West Fife. Local industries would also have benefited from the increased water supply provided by the lake formed behind the dam which would have raised the water level by six feet. This raised water level and the constant high water which it would have ensured would also have benefited the ports of Bo'ness, Grangemouth and Alloa by creating deep water riverside wharfs and doing away with need for ships to wait for daily high tides to enter and leave port. Large locks in the barrage dam were planned to be operational round the clock. Shipbuilding in Grangemouth, always hampered by having to launch newly built vessels sideways into the muddy River Carron would also have benefited and been able to build larger craft.

As a hotelier Jeffrey was particularly enthusiastic that once constant high water hid the Forth's famous mud flats that many more tourists would come to the Forth Lake. A seaplane base for flying boats was planned for Blackness to bring in overseas visitors. Four paddle steamers were to be built to provide summer cruises while a fleet of fast motor launches was planned to provide a year round commuter service to Grangemouth which they foresaw long before their time as Scotland's boom town and site of Central Scotland Airport.

The coming of war in September 1939 stopped not only the passenger flights but also the plans for the barrage dam. By the time peace returned in 1945 campaigning concentrated on a road bridge and in 1964 it was opened interestingly on almost the exact site which Jeffrey and Steele had hoped to utilise for their dam. If they had succeeded Jeffrey and Steele might well have been nationally known names. As it is both are still remembered in their home town as a pair of colourful local characters. Steele's distinctive buildings including the art deco Hippodrome Cinema are more appreciated now than in his own time while a plaque and a local place name, Jeffrey's Corner at the junction of Panbrae Road and the Wynd, recalls his partner John Jeffrey whose Viewforth Hotel, now renamed the Chestnut Lodge, still overlooks the River Forth for which they both had such wonderful plans.

From Jeffrey's Corner the view out over the Forth takes in Low Valleyfield, Preston Island and just beyond it on the Fife shore, the village of Torryburn, two and a half miles east of Culross. Just as Linlithgow possessed Blackness on the south shore as its official outport, so Torryburn was in the past the port for Dunfermline, four and a half miles inland to the north east.

It was during this period that Torryburn was gripped by what was known as the 'witch fever', when its village minister, the Rev Allan Logan appointed himself as the witchfinder general for his parish and devoted himself wholeheartedly to the task of stamping out, 'all trafficking with the Devil and his invisible world'.

Time after time the Rev Mr Logan summoned his kirk session to hear cases of alleged black magic, until in the end one of the old women of the parish, Helen Kay, was brave or foolish enough to voice the opinion of many of the other members of his congregation, that the minister, 'was daft on the witches!'

Furious, Mr Logan had her brought before the session and had her sentenced to be publicly rebuked in front of the whole congregation at the next Sunday worship. Undeterred by old Helen's criticism, Mr Logan continued with his witch trials, the most infamous of which ended in the death of Lilias Adie.

Lilias was arrested by the Baron Bailie of Torryburn in 1704 and was accused of 'being in compact with the Devil'. At her trial Lilias confessed that she had met 'the prince of darkness' on several occasions on the road just outside Torryburn. It is easy to imagine the hushed silence in the court as Lilias was urged by Mr Logan to go on and describe, 'the De'il himself'. With every eye upon her Lilias declared that, 'he was wearing a hat on his head and his feet were cloven, like the feet o' a stirk!'

With this damning evidence given against herself, there could be no other verdict than one of guilty. Normally the Torryburn witches were transported to the Witch Knowe, the hill at

Charlestown, circa 1894. Dunfermline Libraries and Museums.

Dunfermline, where they had their throats wrung and their bodies burned at the stake. No fewer than six women were executed at Dunfermline's Witch Knowe in one six month period. Lilias, however, was saved from such a fate because before she could be transported to the Witch Knowe she died in the jail at Torryburn and as an ex-communicated person was buried on the seashore within the high water mark.

There the tragic story of old Lilias might have ended, but one hundred and ten years ago, her remains were dug up and her skull was purchased by Mr Joseph Paton from Dunfermline. Mr Paton allowed Dr W S Dow to examine it and the doctor wrote the final chapter in her story, when in September 1884, he delivered a lecture to the Fife Medical Association. He informed them that the skull was so abnormally small that he had no hesitation in declaring that poor Lilias had suffered from a diseased brain.

After Torryburn it is necessary to make a detour inland as Crombie Point belongs to the Admiralty and strict security is maintained. Crombie's long pier with its powerful tall cranes is visited regularly by naval transport vessels and is often also used to load frigates and destroyers with their supplies of munitions. During the Falklands War, Crombie set a Royal Naval record for completely provisioning a supplies ship in under twenty four hours.

In contrast to Crombie Point, Charleston is a charming quiet backwater, but it was originally an industrial site. It was founded in 1761 by the sixth Earl of Elgin, whose impressive home Broomhall still stands nearby, to process lime and to export it and

This view of Red Row, Limekilns, is seen from the north-west. Dumfermline Libraries and Museums.

the other products of his estate including limestone, iron ore and coal. Before docks were developed further down river at Burntisland and Methil, Charleston was the main harbour in Fife for the shipping of coal, which went mainly to the Baltic countries, which did not have any supplies of their own. Today its sheltered harbour is still appreciated by local yachtsmen for whom the old Elgin Hotel with its Tavern Bar provides a popular place to recount stories of the day's sailing. Nearby the long 'E' shaped lines of little low cottages in North Row and South Row make a picturesque scene, while Signal Cottage with its unusual ship like architecture is an interesting curiosity.

Dominating the whole waterfront at Charlestown are however the remains of the Elgin Estates massive stone built limekilns in which locally produced coal provided a cheap and plentiful supply of fuel to burn the limestone to produce the white lime for which there was such demand both from agriculture to prepare the fields and from industry for use in the smelting of iron.

Just along the coast delightful little Limekilns also takes its name from the old industry, but it lost its links with it, as Charleston developed. In Victorian times it was hoped that Limekilns' sheltered situation might lead to its development as a holiday resort. This never transpired, but there are few pleasanter spots to sit by the shore on a summer evening and admire the Forth. For those who want to be more active Limekilns and adjoining little

165

The morthouse at Rosyth Burial Ground, near Limekilns, dates from the late 18th or early 19th century, and is now a category B listed building. Dunfermline Libraries and Museums.

Brucehaven are the home of the Forth Cruising Club, whose crow-stepped gabled headquarters is in the village and of the 81st Broomhall Sea Scout Group whose modern but functional headquarters is nearby.

Back on the waterfront the Bruce Arms is yet another reminder of Limekilns' links with the Elgin Estate and it and the Ship Inn are popular places to enjoy a drink by the riverside. The Ship Inn has the added attraction of being the scene chosen by Robert Louis Stevenson for his heroes David Balfour and Allan Breck to dine and drink before being ferried back across the Forth to Queensferry. Adding a splash of Mediterranean colour to the 'Costa Forth', Il Pescators Restaurant offers authentic Italian cuisine and a warm welcome to residents and the many visitors who like to come down to the river and share in the sleepy pleasures which little Limekilns has to offer and in particular its views of the bridges and Queensferry.

CHAPTER 16
THE FERRY

The Royal and Ancient Burgh of Queensferry is one of Scotland's fastest developing towns. The only surprising factor about this is that little Queensferry has not grown up sooner. For with its picturesque setting framed by the two bridges and the fact that it is within such easy reach of Edinburgh, there can be few more attractive places for city businessmen to build their homes and bring up their families. The danger is that having been a slow developer, Queensferry, could become a less than beautiful adolescent with a rash of modern housing spoiling her previously fair complexion.

In 1975 Queensferry was separated from West Lothian by the Wheatley reform of Scottish local government and placed within the Edinburgh District of Lothian Region. Sadly the city fathers never seemed to appreciate this gift of the jewel of the Forth towns. Instead of declaring the whole of Queensferry a conservation area and carefully controlling every development as would have been done with such a historic site in the United States, the Edinburgh councillors happily encouraged the spread of cheap and nasty low budget housing right across the hillside between the bridges and even gave planning permission for a McDonalds fast food outlet, so that now that company's golden arches logo vies for attention with the silver span of the suspension road bridge.

Only now in 1996 is Queensferry receiving some of the attention which such a site of national importance deserves, with a long overdue face-lift for the High Street, with its unique two-tier terraces. Once completed it will make the heart of The Ferry, as it is affectionately known to its inhabitants, a much safer place to walk and happily to explore.

Queensferry takes its name from Queen Margaret, who was later made a saint by a justly appreciative Catholic church. Following the Norman Conquest of England in 1066, the then Princess Margaret and her family, including her mother Queen Agatha and her brother Edgar the Ethling fled from the court in London. The boat on which they were travelling was caught in a fierce storm, blown completely off course and eventually grounded on the south shore of the Forth at what became known as Port Edgar. The royal family immediately enquired the whereabouts of the Scottish royal court and as it was then in Dunfermline, they all, including Margaret, sailed on across the Forth to Fife.

There in the royal palace at Dunfermline Margaret swiftly won the heart of the Scottish king, Malcolm Canmore and within the year they were wed. From then on Queen Margaret wielded great power at the Scottish court and there are many stories of how she used her influence from insisting on the Scottish lords remembering their table manners and stopping throwing bones from the banqueting table to their waiting hounds, to insisting they sew buttons on their sleeves to prevent them wiping their noses with them, a custom still followed on the jackets of mens' suits right down to the present day.

Much more importantly Margaret persuaded King Malcolm and his courtiers to change from worshipping in the fashion of the Celtic Catholic Church to adopt the more modern practices of the Church of Rome. Thus Roman Catholicism came to Scotland and Margaret soon established holy shrines including those at Dunfermline and St Andrews. It was to encourage pilgrims to visit them that the Queen's ferry was first established. To begin with the ferrymen were the monks from Dunfermline Abbey and the point of embarkation on the southside was at the Binks Rocks, right in front of Queensferry's medieval Priory Church of St Mary.

The crossing was often a rough one and one monarch who found it thus was Queen Margaret's son, who later became King Alexander I. In 1123 he was caught in the Forth by a severe gale and was driven ashore on the island of Inchcolm. There he found shelter in a hermit's cell. It can still be seen in the grounds of the Augustinian abbey, which King Alexander founded to show thanks for his rescue from these cruel waters.

Less fortunate was King Alexander III, who reached Queensferry late one dark and stormy night. Despite pleas from the ferrymen to rest for the night and wait to cross at dawn, Alexander, eager to get home to his young French wife in Kinghorn, demanded to be rowed to the Fife shore. Despite the battering from wind and waves they reached the other side, but as the king rode on along the coast in the dark, his horse stumbled and threw him to his death over the cliff at Pettycur, only a mile from his destination at Kinghorn and his true love. His untimely passing plunged Scotland into more years of strife.

By the reign of James VI and I, more peaceful times had come to Scotland, but the weather still caused him trouble when he came to Queensferry in 1617, on his first and only royal visit to Scotland since his accession to the English throne by the Union of the Crowns following the death of Queen Elizabeth in 1603. The river was rough and unwelcoming when the royal party reached the Fife shore, but anxious to reach the comparative civilisation of Holyrood Palace before nightfall, the King embarked. He reached the southern shore in safety, but one of the accompanying fleet of little boats was less fortunate and several of his courtiers and servants were drowned. For years after the accident it was rumoured that a large quantity of the royal silver tableware also went to the bottom, thus creating a Scottish version of how the English King John lost his treasure in the Wash, but despite a recent search, based on Burntisland, nothing of value has ever been found.

By this time after the Reformation of the Scottish church, the Queensferry Passage was no longer operated by the monks, and the rights to the ferry had been divided up into sixteen parts, the owners of which were each entitled to operate one vessel on the crossing. By the beginning of the 17th century the Queen's ferry was the busiest in Scotland, but in 1602 all crossings were banned in an effort to prevent the plague, which was then rampant in Edinburgh, from spreading from the capital to Fife and the north of Scotland. However, the pestilence soon died down and the ferry became its usual busy self once again.

During the 18th century the first turnpike road in Scotland was constructed to link it with Edinburgh, so the idea of paying tolls to use the Forth Road Bridge has a historic precedent. The new turnpike road ran from Edinburgh past Muttonhall, as Davidsons Mains was then known, over Cramond Bridge and out to the Newhalls Inn, as the Hawes at Queensferry was then known. When it was completed it was claimed to be the finest road in Britain, but travellers were less happy with the state of the actual ferry. Their complaints increased steadily after 1784, when the rights to the ferry were put up for annual public auction the new operators being more concerned about recouping their outlay and making a profit within their twelve months of ownership, than about the service they offered. Passengers complained that the piers, especially the one on the south side were in a ruinous condition; that there was no superintendent in charge of the boats; that the ferrymen were often less than sober; and most annoying of all that there were frequent occasions when there were no boats available at the Hawes, because all of the ferrymen had their homes at North Queensferry.

In the end an act of parliament was passed in 1809 appointing trustees to look after the ferry and from then on it was managed in a much more businesslike manner. Not just one but two superintendents were appointed and it was laid down that the boatmen must never be called up to serve in the Royal Navy. The act also stated that no more than two thirds of the boats must be at the same side at any time and a scale of charges was drawn up. For the hire of a small boat by day the charge was half a crown ($12^1/_2$p), but if the traveller left it a little late and arrived after dark the cost doubled and he had to hand over a whole silver crown. Both by day and night, however, certain categories of people escaped paying anything. They included express horsemen carrying the royal mail, soldiers, army and navy volunteers, provided they were in uniform and vagrants, who showed their legal passes.

The biggest change of all to affect the ferry came in 1821 with the introduction for the first time of a steamboat, which was appropriately called, *Queen Margaret*. She was built by Menzies of Leith at a cost of £2,369 and cost twelve pounds and fourteen shillings a week to operate, including the crew's wages! She was regarded as one of the wonders of the age, because not only did she reduce the passage time to only twenty minutes but she was also capable of towing the older sail powered ferries. These were still required to cope with the traffic. The older ferries also retained the advantage that they could sail at all states of the tide, while at low water *Queen Margaret* had to use Longcraig Pier and could not embark stage coaches or any wheeled vehicles from it.

Despite her disadvantages *Queen Margaret* remained in service until 1841. For the last three years of her life on the passage she was used as the spare vessel as a brand new iron hulled steam ferry was built for the crossing in 1838. The newcomer was named *William Adam*, after one of the trustees. The *William Adam* was described in a contemporary account as, 'a very superior seaboat, length ninety eight feet and breadth thirty two, which leaves the south side every hour and the north side every half hour, from sunrise to sunset'. Considering this was still the best service offered up until after the end of the Second World War, this was a considerable achievement. It was not surprising therefore that in 1842 Her Majesty Queen Victoria decided to grace the new Queen's ferry with her presence on one of her journeys to Balmoral. A report of the time records the event as follows. 'The day was most beautiful; the water unruffled, the crowds on both shores very great; the sea covered by numerous steamers and boats, gaily adorned; indeed the whole scene was calculated to make an impression not speedily to be forgotten.'

'It is understood the Sovereign expressed the greatest satisfaction with all the arrangements made on board the steamer. Mr Mason, the superintendent, took the helm, while the attentive skipper Charles Roxburgh, attended to the other duties.'

Not all crossings during Queen Victoria's reign went so smoothly. Only four years earlier there had been a tragedy on the Hawes Pier, when in October 1838 a coach crashed off it, into the water. Despite the frantic efforts of the ferrymen, the young woman and her female servant who were the sole occupants, were both drowned before they were pulled free.

The coming of the railways to Scotland in the 1840s had a major effect on the ferry. A parliamentary act in 1848 gave the trustees the power to let the passage to the new Edinburgh and Glasgow Railway Company, but this was never implemented and soon the lack of a railway connection began to affect business. That same year the opening of a new steam ferry from Granton to Burntisland where it connected with the trains of the Edinburgh, Perth and Dundee Railway Company had a devastating effect on the amount of traffic passing through Queensferry.

In the end the railway finally reached Dalmeny in 1866, a branch line being constructed from the main one at Ratho. Three years later the line was extended north to a new station called Newhalls on the high ground to the west of the Hawes Inn, from where porters were laid on to carry luggage up and down to the pier, but this was always considered second best to a much more ambitious scheme to restore Queensferry's fortunes by operating a train ferry from Port Edgar. A railway line was laid, but the building of a train ferry to connect with it was delayed by a plan to do away with the need for it by building a railway bridge across the river from Blackness to Charleston. While all this wrangling went on the ferry trustees went bankrupt. The operation of the ferry was rescued by the owner of Scotland's last fleet of stage coaches, John Croall. For the next nine years the ferry carried Croall's famous coach, *Antiquary* on her daily run to and from Dunfermline. It became the last stage coach to maintain a regular service in Scotland and it too ended upon Croall's death in 1873.

By then the rights to the ferry had been purchased by the North British Railway Company and in 1877 they introduced a new ferry named, *John Beaumont* after one of its directors. Although purpose built for the passage by John Key of Kinghorn, the new boat proved inadequate to cope with the tides and currents on the crossing and two years later was replaced by the *Thane of Fife*, which was transferred from the Granton to Burntisland route.

Despite this improvement the ferry at Queensferry was never busy and trade decreased still further with the opening of the Forth Bridge in 1890. The North British Railway Company no longer wanted the ferry, but had a legal obligation dating back to their purchase of the rights, to maintain a minimum service. This they did by leasing the rights first to Captain John Arthur and later to John Wilson, the Bo'ness tugmaster, and providing them with a small subsidy to operate the required sailings.

Then in the early 1900s the fortunes of the Queensferry Passage began to change, because of the arrival of the newfangled motor cars and a steady growth in road traffic. This increased greatly with the start of the First World War in 1914, mainly because of Admiralty work in connection with the new naval base which was being brought into use across the water at Rosyth.

John Wilson died shortly after the end of the war and during the 1920s the railway company was forced to operate the ferry service on its own as it could not find anyone else to lease it. To do so they brought the former Tay ferry *Dundee* to the Forth. She was already forty five years old when she first arrived at Queensferry and by the start of the 1930s the steady increase in cars waiting to cross the river, showed up her inadequacies even more. Angry motorists demanded that the service be improved, but as the depression worsened the railway company, which had by this time become incorporated in the famous LNER, was reluctant to invest. It was at this time that fortunately for Queensferry the shrewd and far sighted Scottish shipbuilder, Sir Maurice Denny hove on the scene.

Desperate for business to keep his skilled workforce occupied during the years of the depression Sir Maurice appealed to the railway company to give him the order for two super-ferries. Cautious of putting their shareholders at risk during the recession of the 1930s the directors of the LNER refused, but instead offered to lease him the rights to operate the passage, if he would finance the building of the boats.

Sir Maurice accepted the gamble and for the next three years, while other Clydeside shipbuilding yards were laying off more and more men, those employed by Denny of Dumbarton were kept busy building the two new ferries for the Forth.

As he was building them for his own firm Sir Maurice was free to build them to his own design. The side loading of the earlier ferries was retained as it worked well because it allowed them to cope with the considerable tidal rise and fall at the piers on both sides of the river.

More surprisingly, paddle power was also retained, but the Denny designed electric propulsion for the paddles was much more efficient and made the new ferries much more manoeuvrable than any other vessel of the period.

Equally revolutionary was the hull design of both vessels as they were built with bows at both ends and car decks completely clear of any obstructions, apart from two small cabins at either end, one for foot passengers and the other to provide quarters for the crew.

The central overhead bridge was designed to provide clearance for even the highest furniture pantechnicon, which was the largest type of vehicle on the roads of the 1930s.

Sir Maurice also took the opportunity to try a controlled experiment on the then new process of electric welding. The *Robert the Bruce* was built entirely using this method while the *Queen Margaret* was constructed using traditional welding methods so that the yard could study the pros and cons of electric welding on two vessels operating under identical conditions.

Both *Queen Margaret* and the *Robert the Bruce* were launched together in March 1934 at a double ceremony at Dumbarton and as soon as they arrived at Queensferry were put onto a thirty minute service, the first time this had been achieved on the passage on a regular basis since almost a century previously in the 1840s.

The establishment of the new service was however not without controversy because although fares were halved to between five and eleven shillings depending on the size of car, the Fife Roads Board still protested that they were too high. There was a prolonged correspondence in Scotland's top daily newspaper *The Scotsman*, but Sir Maurice refused to reduce fares, arguing that the levels he had set were necessary to ensure a return on his firm's investment. A 20% concession was however agreed for commercial travellers. To add to the row shortly after entering service the *Queen Margaret* had to be withdrawn from service to undergo minor repairs and alterations at the Grangemouth Dock Company's Carron Dry Dock and no sooner was she back on station than the *Robert The Bruce* grounded off the Hawes Pier at South Queensferry.

After these teething troubles, however, the distinctive pair in their smart black and white livery became a familiar sight shuttling to and fro beneath the railway bridge and became very popular with drivers, who were impressed by their reliability. Together they maintained the service for fifteen years, right through the Second World War and on until 1949. After peace was declared in 1945 the campaign for a new road bridge was intensified and in 1947 parliament passed a bill agreeing that one should be built, but Maurice Denny decided on another calculated gamble.

He was convinced that with post-war shortages it would be so long before a road bridge spanned the Forth that it would be worth his company's while to build a third ferry to cope with the ever increasing traffic, which the relaxation of war time petrol rationing was already bringing.

The original design of the *Queen Margaret* and *Robert the Bruce* had worked so successfully that the *Mary Queen of Scots* was built to almost exactly the same design and her addition to the little fleet meant that a twenty minute service could be introduced.

Even with this big improvement in service the queues of cars continued to grow and as the rows about a tunnel or a road bridge continued to rage, throughout the early 1950s Sir Maurice decided that the demand justified a fourth ferry.

Keeping up the tradition of Scottish historical names, the *Sir William Wallace* arrived at Queensferry in 1955. She was slightly larger than her three earlier sisters and her introduction meant that with improvements to the Hawes Pier and to the pier at North

Queensferry, it became possible to introduce a fifteen minute service at peak times.

By then the number of passengers had grown to over two million and the number of vehicles to 90,000 annually. Two hour waits became not uncommon and Sir Maurice was about to commission a fifth larger ferry from Dennys, when at last in 1958 work began on the new road bridge.

The fifth ferry was never built. Six years later on 4th September 1964 the Forth Road Bridge was finally officially opened by Her Majesty the Queen. On that foggy Friday morning the sun broke through the sea fret just as she and the Duke of Edinburgh drove over the shining new silver suspension bridge, the 'highway in the sky', as it was nicknamed at the time, which was to put an end to the 900 year old Queensferry Passage.

Appropriately, however, Her Majesty made her return journey by ferry and even more appropriately the honour of transporting the Queen was bestowed on the *Queen Margaret*, which had sailed the route for all of thirty years. Two days later it was also the *Queen Margaret*, which made the very last crossing. Limited to passengers only, a short religious service was held on her now deserted car deck just before she tied up at the Hawes Pier for the final time.

Unfortunately Scottish tourism was not as developed in the 1960s as it is now and the opportunity to retain at least one of the ferries to operate pleasure cruises below the two bridges was not seized. Instead the four familiar black and white ferries, so beloved and at other times depending on wind, weather and waiting times, hated by Scottish motorists and lorry drivers were sold for scrap in the case of the first three, while the newer *Sir William Wallace* was sold to foreign owners in the Netherlands and so sailed away into history.

Over thirty years later the Hawes Pier has surprisingly recovered much of its activities with several vessels plying from its long sloping quays. Throughout the year it is the base for the private ferries which sail to and from British Petroleum's Hound Island oil terminal just down river from the Forth Bridge. An underwater pipe line connects the terminal with Dalmeny Tank Farm and fuel is pumped direct into the giant hundred thousand ton tankers which moor alongside its two berths and when loaded carry their cargoes to the international spot oil market in

Rotterdam. Hound Island takes its name from Hound Point, the basalt promontory in front of Barnbougle Castle on Lord Rosebery's Dalmeny Estate, which is said to be haunted by the ghost of a hunting dog. The hound had accompanied its master Sir Rodger de Mowbray of Barnbougle when he went to fight on a Crusade to the Holy Land. There he was slain by a Saracen Turk and on dark winter nights when gales lash the shores of the Forth, the ghostly hound is said to be accompanied by the spectre of a white clad Arab warrior, as it howls balefully from the rocks as it seeks in vain for its slaughtered master.

Back at the Hawes Pier, however, it is on summer days that it has really come back into its own with regular sailings by the *Maid of the Forth* down river to Inchcolm to visit its ancient abbey, inspect its tunnel and other First and Second World War installations, see the seals basking on its rocks and hopefully even spot the puffins hiding on its grassy slopes. During holiday periods there is even a passenger only ferry across to Town Pier, North Queensferry.

The pier is also kept busy as a venue for powerboat owners and water-ski and sailboard enthusiasts, whose activities add colour to the scene. On occasions, of course, all these water sport participants also add to the work of Queensferry's lifeboat crew whose headquarters at the pierhead is often open to visitors to inspect their semi rigid inflatable and at the same time boost much needed funds for the Royal National Lifeboat Institute.

Also at the landward end of the Hawes can still be seen the town's lighthouse designed around 1810 by Robert Stevenson, grandfather of the famous author. Several plans have been put forward to restore this old building, but at present its sandstone is sadly crumbling, especially on its west facade, the side nearest the town from which the prevailing wind whips the salt sea spray. Perhaps a start could be made by asking the many tourists who like to stroll down the Hawes especially when the tide is out, to make a small contribution to save this part of the pier's history.

Someone who added much to the colourful nature of the history of the Hawes, at least in fiction, was Robert Louis Stevenson, who perhaps inspired by his grandfather's links with the place, chose it as the setting for his hero David Balfour's abduction in his famous novel, *Kidnapped*. Prior to the actual kidnap one of the most important scenes in the book is also set in

The famous Hawes Inn is situated right below the Forth Bridge. Ian Torrance.

the famous Hawes Inn immediately opposite the pier, when the wily old Uncle Ebeneezer uses one of its upstairs rooms to introduce Davy to the skipper of the barque on which the plan is to carry him away to a life of white slavery. The Hawes now displays many pictures of the characters from *Kidnapped*, but it should not be forgotten that the old whitewashed inn at the foot of New Halls Brae, from which it derives its name, also inspired Sir Walter Scott to feature it in his novel, *The Antiquary*.

The Hawes was formerly a popular stage coach halt, while passengers waited for the ferry and in its former stables and coachhouses are now situated several interesting small businesses including the Queensferry Cooperage. Coopers have a long tradition of working in The Ferry, because of the old royal burgh's long connection in the past with whisky distilling, but the cooperage now concentrates on producing small barrels for decorative and garden use.

Away from the Hawes the Esplanade stretches away towards the Seals Craig. It is strange to think that until the opening of the road bridge, cars used to queue here in lines two to three deep waiting patiently or impatiently for the ferry to carry them across the river. Cresting the brae at the Seals Craig the road narrows dramatically from the wide sweep of the 1930s concrete Esplanade into the history steeped High Street. No seals now sun themselves on the rocks this far up river, but it is good to know they are flourishing only a few miles down river. Perhaps there is even hope that as the Forth Conservation Board progressively cleans up the river, that they may return.

In the High Street its unique Terraces offer a choice of levels to explore. Surely one of these fine 18th-century terraced houses must have been the one Stevenson imagined as the home of the lawyer to whom David Balfour returned after his Highland adventures. Certainly the even older early 17th century Black Castle deserves a story told about it, because this was the headquarters of Queensferry's smugglers and by tradition an underground passage linked it to the shore opposite, through which they could roll their kegs of brandy and carry their boxes of cigars and bales of fine silks.

Nose behind the houses of the Terraces, venture up the steps, through the closes and wynds and discover Queensferry's original plain unadorned parish kirk. The lieges of Queensferry paid for it to be built in 1633 so that they and, 'the numberous traders and merchants frequenting the Burgh should not be deprived of the Sacraments'. In 1633 it was declared a parish church by King Charles II, who paid his only royal visit to Scotland in that same year and was consecrated in 1635 by David Lindsay, Bishop of Edinburgh. Its bell was brought across the North Sea from Holland. It is inscribed, 'Soli Deo Gloria Michael Burgerhuys Me Fecit. David Jonking Maerchant of Edinburgh Gifted This bell To The Kirk Of Queensferrie. Cursed Be They That Takes It Frae There. Anno Domini 1635'. Sadly the kirk is now no longer in use, its members having merged with the other Church of Scotland congregation and worshipping in its modern church at the top of the Loan which does not even have a bell. Behind the original oblong 17th-century kirk lies its graveyard and the inscriptions on many of its tombstones tell much about life in Queensferry in past centuries.

Much of that life revolved around the town's tight little harbour. Today it is full of pleasure craft, but in the past it was a hive of business, especially in the fishing season. Every year the Ferry fishermen used to say, 'They'll be up to pay the rent', meaning that the little silver sprats would swim up the Forth in their gleaming millions every November thus ensuring they would have enough to pay their rents at term time on the 28th day of that month. Today the tiny sprats, which are little cousins of the herring, are usually thought only fit for fish-meal for animal feed, but in the 18th and 19th century there was great demand for these little fish for salting. By the thousand they were stuffed into wooden barrels and exported to Germany, Denmark, Norway and Sweden and the profits provided a rich sea harvest not just for the fishermen, but for everyone else involved in the trade from the fisher lassies who followed the sprats around the coast to gut and salt them, to the carters who came to transport them.

Not everyone welcomed the November invasion, however, for the catches as well as ensuring money to pay the rent, also provided plenty of extra siller and according to reports at the time, much of this was spent on strong drink. Parish minister Thomas Dimma deplored the effect all this alcohol had on the morals of his flock. Writing in the Second Statistical Account of Scotland he stated, 'Though this fish trade is most beneficial to the country at large, it is not favourable to the morality of the town. Forty or fifty carters are frequently in attendance and the consumption of ardent spirits is greatly increased. The carters, who are not generally of the most exemplary character cast a bad influence around the fishing season, which is most injurious to sound morals'.

The minister's moral concerns were also added to by the arrival of large numbers of fishermen, who hastened from other ports to share in the catch and even more so by the crowds of fisher lassies, who followed them to gut and salt the wee silver sprats. Mr Dimma estimated as many as a hundred fishing boats crowded into Queensferry's tiny port. In an attempt to lessen the crush on the high stone quays onto which the fish were landed, the tax on each barrel of sprats or 'garvies' as they were known locally, was reduced from four pence if cured on the harbour side to only two pence if carted up into the town for gutting and salting.

Once the day's work was over, however, no matter where the sprats had been processed, the girls joined the fishermen and the carters in Queensferry's, 'one inn, eight ale houses and four shops with accommodation provided for drinking', which according to the Rev Mr Dimma were, 'all most prejudicial to the morals of the people'. The minister then continued, 'Accidents of a most frightful character have occurred almost every year from the immoderate use of spirits and though there have been deaths both by fire and water, the votaries of dissipation are neither improved nor diminished in number'. In the end Queensferry's problems with its yearly November fishing invasion were solved by the sprats themselves, because for some unexplained reason by the close of the 19th century, they no longer arrived in the river in such numbers.

One aspect of Queensferry, however, which has not changed is its numerous drinking places, but today, they've gone up market from the Moorings at the west end of the High Street to the Ferry Tap in the east and been joined by many good quality hotels and restaurants catering for the tourists, who love exploring the old burgh. The hotels range from the traditional Queensferry Arms, with its Arrol Suite named after the bridge designer, the Seals Craig and the Hawes all with wonderful views of the river to the modern Moat House which in addition to its river outlook offers the latest in leisure facilities from a swimming pool to a 'high tech' gymnasium. Plans are also in place for another new hotel overlooking the Road Bridge roundabout. Already in addition to the dining rooms offered by all the hotels, visitors have the choice of several good eating places including the Boat House, with its interesting setting in a converted boat builder's right on the shore, to the roof top opportunities to enjoy French cuisine at Pierre Victoire's.

There are also several cafes and even the Bridges Book Store offers a tearoom with home baking. While a bookshop is to be welcomed in any high street, the one regret in the case of the Bridges Book Store is that it replaced the famous Nardini's ice-cream shop and fish restaurant, which occupied this site in the Terraces for most of this century. The Nardinis were one of several Italian immigrant families who introduced these complementary summer and winter tastes of ice-cream and fish and chips to towns throughout the Forth Valley. Most famous undoubtedly were the Fortes, whose son Charles opened a cafe in Alloa and went on to become head of the world's largest hotel chain, Trust House Forte. Others have remained locally including the Serafinis in Falkirk and Bo'ness in the latter of which they compete with the Corvis, and the Cabrellis of Linlithgow, the Bonis of Bathgate and The Lucas of Musselburgh.

Opposite where Nardini in Queensferry used to fry their haddock and chips and sell their cones, wafers and in a less politically correct age their popular extra special, 'black men', vanilla ice-cream sandwiched between two chocolate nougat wafers, another building which has seen several changes of uses is the former municipal headquarters, the Burgh Chambers. The old building, whose foundations are lapped by the tides was originally the appropriately named Viewforth Hotel. It was later taken over as the seat of administration of Queensferry's Town Council in the days when each Scottish town had its own town clerk, treasurer and burgh surveyor and looked after its own immediate affairs, some would say in a much more efficient manner than subsequent larger local authorities, which have lacked the local touch.

At the beginning of the 1940s at the start of the Second World War, Queensferry's Burgh Chambers suddenly found greatness thrust upon it when it became the royal headquarters of Prince Olaf, Crown Prince of Norway and his fellow naval officers and it was from there that they planned the downfall of the Nazis who had invaded their country and its ultimate liberation in 1945. Even during the darkest days of the war, the loyal Norwegians never forgot their prince in exile and each Christmas a small Norwegian Christmas tree was smuggled across the North Sea and its candles lit in the blacked-out council chambers, as a little reminder of his homeland. After peace was won in 1945, the Norwegians never forgot what Scotland had done for them during World War Two and ever since have gifted a tall, proud Norwegian Fir, shipped across the North Sea by Christian Salvesen of Leith to become Edinburgh's Christmas tree high on the Mound overlooking the city and the River Forth beyond.

After the war Queensferry's Burgh Chambers returned to their local government use, until the disbandment of the Town Council and the take over by Lothian Regional Council and Edinburgh District Council in 1975. The disused chambers have now been converted into the Burgh Museum with displays about the two bridges and Queensferry's many links with the Forth. The largest exhibit is however a reminder of one of the building's former roles as the burgh court, in the shape of the town's whipping block, over which any local juvenile delinquents, who broke the law in the years up until 1947, were made to bend to receive corporal punishment. The soli dly constructed wooden block with its padded top is equipped with stout leather straps to ensure the erring youths were held firm to ensure their bottoms received the full effect of the number of strokes of the birch rod to which they had been sentenced by the burgh's bailies.

While deterrence by birching is a thing of the past and unlikely to return because of the interference by the European Court of Human Rights, another aspect of Queensferry life, which still continues is also well illustrated in the museum through a colourful display on the famous Burry Man. It is sometimes suggested this strange figure takes his name from the burgh through which he parades, but it seems more likely he is named after the coat of sticky green burrs from the burdock plant with which every inch of him is covered from the top of his head to the tips of his toes. One local legend is that the Burry Man originated as a ship wrecked mariner washed up on the shore at Port Edgar and some even connect the event with the coming of Prince Edgar and his sister Princess Margaret in 1069. The legend continues that having lost all his clothes in the storm the Burry Man originally covered himself in burrs to cover his embarrassment and modesty before venturing into Queensferry to find help. This is said to tie in with the Burry Man's right to this day to collect money from every person he meets on his perambulations through the town.

The Burry Man's other privilege is to claim a kiss from every pretty girl, no matter how young or old, he meets during the day and this suggests another probable origin as a fertility symbol thus making him Scotland's answer to England's mysterious Green Man. The elaborate floral bonnet worn by the Burry Man and the equally brilliantly colourful flower decorated staffs which he carries in each hand also suggest a fertility rites origin, as does the time of year that he makes his annual appearance. For it is as the fields around Queensferry turn to August ripe harvest gold that the Burry Man's followers take to the slopes of the shale bings around Dalmeny and hunt the hedgerows around The Newton and Hopetoun to gather the thousands and thousands of small green burrs required to make his costume on the Friday before the Ferry Fair. Rising as soon as dawn breaks the Burry Man puts on woollen long-john style underpants, a woollen high necked long sleeved semmit or vest and a knitted balaclava helmet, ready for his supporters to begin the painstaking task of creating his unique green suit. In years past, without realising it, the Burry Man's dressers were probably the discoverers of the principle on which space age velcro is based. Finally the Burry Man is crowned with his floral headpiece and has a gold and scarlet lion rampant flag wrapped round his waist as a cumberband. Then with his flower decorated wooden staffs in his hands the Burry Man is ready for his once yearly appearance in the streets of Queensferry.

Accompanied by his collectors rattling their tins for contributions to the well deserved pints of beer, which they will later share, the Burry Man acts as a magnet for the town's children, who follow him Pied Piper like down the Loan, along the length of the High Street and onto the Esplanade, where visitors from home and abroad throng to see and photograph this bizarre sight. The Burry Man's walkabout continues throughout the day until the sun sets over the span of the suspension bridge, but at the other end of the town the revelry continues on into the night at the annual funfair at the Hawes. There the shows do a brisk trade and the multicoloured lights of the stalls and rides reflect in the dark waters of the Forth, as they wash against the Esplanade.

When the Ferry folk eventually sleep it is not for long, because come daybreak they are up again to prepare for the Ferry Fair. Nowadays the highlight of the proceedings is the mid-morning coronation of the town's school girl queen, who is chosen each summer in turn from each of the burgh's three primary schools, Echline, Queensferry and St Margaret's and her crowning in an impressive ceremony held in front of the old Burgh Chambers overlooking the river, but older traditions are also still kept up. These include the Burgh race round the boundaries of the town and the High Street race with its prize of a pair of boots. Later in the day at the sports in the Burgess Park local youngsters still attempt to slither to the top of the greasy pole, with its memories of the days when their forebears climbed the masts and rigging of the sailing boats in the harbour.

From the harbour narrow lanes lead up to the High Street. One of them is called Covenanters Lane and is a reminder of the years in the 17th century when leading members of the religious movement faced with persecution from the government forces, used to find safe shelter in the crowded homes around the harbour until a ship was ready to sail on the next tide to carry them across the North Sea to temporary sanctuary in Protestant Holland. There they waited until the time was right for them to return to Scotland to fight again for their cause. One house where they often hid was called Queen Margaret's Palace. Up from the harbour too is the little square off the High Street, where the stone carved with the

Bell Stane Bird is situated. It is from it that just as the people of Falkirk are known as the 'Bairns', the people of Grangemouth, 'Portonians' and the residents of Bo'ness used to be called 'Garvies' after the wee sprats, so the residents of Queensferry are dubbed 'Bell Stane Birds'.

Amongst them must have been the residents of Plewlands House, Queensferry's oldest occupied building, which stands opposite the Bell Stane Square on the corner at the foot of the Loan. A fine typically Scottish 'L' shaped mansion with a twisting newel stair, it has been well restored by the National Trust. It is not open to the public as it has been converted into a number of private flats.

The Loan leads up the hill, past the site on the left where Trafalgar Cottage used to stand and on the right the Co-operative Supermarket, which occupies part of the grounds formerly occupied by what was at the time the town's largest industry, the old distillery. At one time the distillery, which was owned by the Distillers' Agency Ltd employed over five hundred workers. Later it was converted into a blending and bottling plant processing the popular VAT 69. The distillery was very badly damaged by a spectacular blaze in 1949 during which many barrels exploded and burst with the fierce heat sending a river of flaming whisky pouring down the Loan. Fire appliances from Edinburgh and all parts of West Lothian fought the blaze and after the fire was put out a large part of the distillery had to be demolished. It was rebuilt in red brick and reopened in 1952. The 'VAT' as it was affectionately known in the town was finally closed in 1985 and most of its buildings were demolished.

The closure of the distillery cost several hundred jobs, but fortunately by then Queensferry had moved into the new-age world of electronic industry. First to open in 1966 was the micro-electronics plant of Hewlett-Packard. Situated on top of the hill behind the High Street near Dalmeny Railway Station the factory was greatly extended in 1989 until now Hewlett-Packard has a work force of more than one thousand people. It has been joined on the western outskirts of the town by a second giant electronics plant, developed first by Digital and now owned by the very successful Motorola Company.

Queensferry's other former major employer was Port Edgar Royal Naval Base. It was purchased at the start of the First World

War by the Admiralty, thus continuing the navy's long connections with the town, which dated back to Victorian times. Whereas formerly the ships of the fleet anchored off the town in the river, the purchase of Port Edgar provided a base for sixty-six destroyers and auxiliary vessels. In addition to their ship's companies totalling five thousand officers and men, at the height of the war, Port Edgar employed one thousand dockyard workers at a time when Rosyth across the river was still being built. For Queensferry it was a rich war, with accommodation at a premium and local shops doing a roaring trade supplying the fleet.

The boom ended in the 1920s, partly because of the development of Rosyth but also because of the depression throughout the country as a whole. In 1927 matters were made even worse when Port Edgar was reduced to a care and maintenance basis. During the 1930s some of the naval barracks were used as holiday accommodation for unemployed families from Edinburgh and Glasgow and school children also attended several camps, a use which was suggested again in the 1980s for the building known as the Norwegian Block.

In 1939 with the start of the Second World War, Port Edgar was hurriedly recommissioned as a land-based training school known as HMS *Lochinvar*, where the crews of minesweepers were trained. Minesweepers had wooden hulls and several of the vessels based at Port Edgar were built locally at Thomson and Balfour's Victoria and Links Sawmills at Bo'ness, where MTBs, motor torpedo boats were also constructed.

HMS *Lochinvar* was the Royal Navy's only minesweeping training school and it also served as the sea base for the testing of all new mine disposal gear. In addition to its own officers and crew the Royal Navy at Port Edgar also trained thousands of foreign sailors for the war effort. They came mainly from Norway and Belgium, but one group of trawlermen travelled to it all the way from the Falkland Islands. HMS *Lochinvar* was paid special recognition for the part it was playing in the war when in 1941 amidst intense security King George VI paid a secret visit to the base.

In addition to the minesweeping base at Port Edgar, the former naval hospital, a short distance to the west at Butlaw, was again revived and greatly expanded, while Butlaw Camp was reopened as extra barracks. All this naval activity again ensured Queensferry prospered, but after the war Port Edgar slowly declined until it was finally closed as a naval base in 1975.

In May 1976 it was purchased by Lothian Regional Council for development as a yachting marina and a water sports training school. Port Edgar offers the only real marina facilities on the Forth with walk-on pontoon berths usable at all states of the tide and supplied with electricity and water supplies. Ashore there is plenty of space for the parking of yachts and dinghies, while around one hundred and fifty small vessels can be stored under cover in large hangars and sheds. A fixed crane on the central pier can lift craft up to five tons and the concrete slipway is usable at most states of the tide. Port Edgar also has a busy ships' chandlers known as the Bosun's Locker and a cafe, appropriately called The Galley, which is open everyday throughout the summer and at weekends during the rest of the year. It often has many hungry mouths to feed as in addition to local sailing enthusiasts who keep their vessels at Port Edgar, the marina also often welcomes many visiting craft including many from abroad and the sailing school also attracts lots of learners, both young and older.

Port Edgar is an ideal place to learn water sports as the huge sheltered harbour provides plenty of space for beginners, while the open river below the Forth Road Bridge provides more exciting water for those who have progressed further. Courses available include instruction in all levels of sailing dinghies, learning to canoe and opportunities to try sailboarding and even how to man powered rescue craft. For those who are already competent sailors Port Edgar offers a fleet of dinghies and sailboards for hire, including little Mirrors, ideal for children, Toppers, GP14s and Wayfarers. The port is also the home base for the pleasure vessel *Maid of the Forth* and the Forth River Purification Board's patrol and research vessel, *Rover*. The Board's headquarters and laboratories are at Heriot-Watt Research Park, Riccarton.

Port Edgar has certainly come a long way from the deserted shore on which its name sake Prince Edgar and Princess Margaret first stepped ashore.

CHAPTER 17
THE BRIDGES

Port Edgar, its yachts and dinghies are all dwarfed by the span of the Forth Road Bridge, which sweeps high overhead. The slender, streamlined, silver road bridge is in marked contrast to the mighty, massive, muckle railway bridge down river to the east, yet each seems to compliment the other, symbols of the two different centuries in which they were built.

While the world famous rail bridge predates the road bridge by three quarters of a century, it is interesting to note that the earliest project to span the river at this point was for a road crossing. Detailed plans for this early crossing were drawn up in 1818 by James Anderson, an Edinburgh engineer, who proposed the construction of a chain suspension bridge. His bridge was to have had a twenty five feet (approximately eight metres) wide carriageway with footpaths for pedestrians on either side. The main spans were to have been 1500 feet (475 metres) long and were to have been manufactured of Swedish steel, treated with linseed oil, which Mr Anderson claimed would prevent rust and therefore do away with the need for painting. American oak was to be used for the roadway, which was to be surfaced with a mixture of gravel, sand and chalk, bound together with pitch and tar. While Anderson had done his homework well, he had chosen a bad time to put forward his proposals, which he costed at £175,000. They were rejected as much too costly for the country to fund, 'as it was still impoverished following the long war with Napoleon'.

A road bridge was not the only alternative canvassed for the ferry during the nineteenth century. Several Victorian engineers drew up plans for a tunnel, but the two hundred feet depth of the channels on either side of Inchgarvie Island were a daunting challenge.

The coming of the railways increased the pressure for the building of a bridge, because of the obvious gap in Scotland's otherwise fast improving communications network, which the Forth was proving. At the same time as the construction of the original Tay Bridge in the 1870s plans were drawn up for a similar railway aqueduct to span the Forth. The Tay Bridge disaster on the night of Sunday 28th December 1879, after it had been in use for only two years, forced a complete rethink and it was decided the solution to spanning the even more windswept waters of the Forth would be to build a revolutionary cantilever design.

For two years at the beginning of the 1880s Sir Benjamin Baker, who was granted his knighthood for his efforts, carried out wind pressure tests on both sides of the river. At the end of them he stated that the results proved the pressure of 56lb per square foot laid down for the design for the Forth Bridge by the committee set up after the Tay tragedy, 'was considerably in excess of anything likely to be realised'. With this assurance instructions were given for the work to commence in 1893. The job was entrusted to Tancred, Arrol and Company and like Baker, William Arrol was later knighted for creating what was to become one of the modern wonders of the world.

A total workforce of 4,600 men was recruited. Some came from Scotland but the project acted like a magnet for unemployed labourers from much further afield and many came from Ireland and others from even farther away from Northern Italy, Austria, Germany, Belgium and France. Most were accommodated not at Queensferry, but in long lines of wooden huts at Kirkliston, which although further away allowed easier access as the men could be transported to work by train along the Ratho to Dalmeny branch line. At the time the basic diet of the Irishmen earned Kirkliston the nickname of 'Cheesetown', because of the vast quantities of the stuff ordered and consumed each week during the seven years, which the enormous enterprise took to complete.

With such a vast labour force it was not surprising that during such a long period there was occasionally industrial unrest and there were several strikes. The most serious lasted just over a week and occurred in June 1897 shortly after an accident had resulted in the deaths of three of the workmen. In all around five hundred of the men were injured and fifty seven lives were lost during the building of the Forth Bridge, but there is no truth in the story that several of the labourers were trapped at the foot of one of the cantilevers and when they could not be rescued that poisoned food was sent down to put them out of their misery.

In the building of the bridge 51,000 tons of Siemens-Martin steel

The cantilever design of the Forth Bridge is displayed to advantage in this picture. Ian Torrance.

forged by the open hearth method and the strongest in the world was used and all of it was fabricated in enormous workshops constructed on the shore at Queensferry. In addition the bridge required 140,000 cubic feet of granite for the massive piers used to support the steel girders. One of Sir William Arrol's most ingenious ideas was not to wait until the stone pillars reached full height before laying the girders but to allow the pillars to carry them up using hydraulic power and this saved a great deal of time and money. The system adopted for the building of the piers was to construct large cylinders of wrought iron called caissons which were supplied with compressed air. Six of these pneumatic caissons were built and carefully sunk in position in the river under the guidance of Monsieur Coiseau, a French engineer who was the world expert in this form of sub-aquatic construction.

Once the caissons were safely on the bed of the river, workmen were ferried out and descended into them to start the excavations, the river water being kept out by pumping in compressed air. A contemporary account states, 'In order to allow of the requisite air pressure being maintained the top of the shafts were closed by air locks, which may be described as an arrangement of double doors, one of which was always kept closed. Light was obtained from incandescent electric lamps and as the excavation proceeded, the caisson was forced down by gradual additions of concrete. The excavated material was removed through shafts. Upon the foundations thus formed the granite piers were constructed and carried up to a height of eighteen feet above high-water mark. The steel lower bed-plates for the support of the cantilever central towers rested on their tops and were firmly secured by massive steel bolts, built into the stone work'.

The account continues, 'The construction of the great steel columns forming the central towers was effected by means of moveable platforms surrounding and attached to the columns. These platforms supported the workmen and all the necessary appliances for placing and rivetting the curved steel plates and which were raised by hydraulic power as the work progressed. This was a sufficiently remarkable mode of procedure, but that of constructing the members of the cantilevers, horizontally for a distance of six hundred and eighty feet in mid-air, without any support whatsoever from below, was still more astonishing. However thanks to the skill and determination of the contractors and their workmen this feat was also accomplished by the same means of moveable platforms suspended from the members and gradually advanced as the work proceeded'.

The chief engineer during the whole of the construction of the bridge was Sir John Fowler and under his supervision the massive bridge like a giant Meccano set inched towards completion. As soon as the three huge cantilevers were constructed the work of constructing the central girders began and at length the central portion of the two girders met one hundred and fifty feet above the river and were rivetted together on 7th November 1889.

There was, however, a considerable amount of minor work chiefly in connection with the internal viaducts still remaining to be finished and it was not until February 1890 that the bridge was ready for inspection by officials of the Board of Trade. Their report read, 'This great undertaking every part of which we have seen at different stages of its construction, is a wonderful example of thoroughly good workmanship, with excellent materials and both in its conception and execution is a credit to all who have been connected with it'.

The Forth Bridge was officially opened on 4th March 1890 by Queen Victoria's eldest son, Edward the Prince of Wales. The royal train steamed out from the Queensferry side and halted right in the centre of the bridge. There the Crown Prince descended onto the track and drove home the last of the bridge's six and a half million rivets. Originally it was intended to use a gold rivet to mark the occasion, but money was so scarce by this point in the construction that, without His Royal Highness's knowledge, a brass one was substituted instead. Funds did however stretch to providing a royal feast for Edward and all the other distinguished guests, who included Monsieur Eiffel, the designer of the famous Parisian tower.

A special commemorative card gives the Forth Bridge's statistics as, '$1^3/_4$ miles long, including its approaches; 361 feet tall at its highest point above sea level with 150 feet of clearance below its spans at high water. It utilised 51,000 tons of steel, has foundations going down to a depth of 91 feet below high water mark and cost £3 million'.

Almost immediately the work of maintaining the bridge began using a paint specially created by the famous Scottish firm of Craig and Rose, Paint Manufacturers of 172 Leith Walk, Edinburgh and its russet colour has become so famous that it has become known as Forth Bridge Red. Until the economies of the 1990s, when a year went past without any painting, a team of painters has been employed continuously working on the bridge, thus introducing into the English language the saying, 'It's just like painting the Forth Bridge' to describe a job that seems to go on and on and on for ever. The famous Forth Bridge painters even have their own aerial bothy just below the level of the railway tracks, in which to spend their tea breaks and eat their meals, so that they do not have to come down until the end of their shifts. Whenever men are working on the bridge, a safety boat, based at the North Queensferry side, patrols the waters of the Forth beneath the bridge in case of accidents.

Unlike its newer neighbour the road bridge, the rail bridge has never been equipped with remote control television cameras, but until recently it was manned twenty four hours a day and a night patrol ensured there has never been any vandalism or terrorist attack. Very early on however in the 1890s, Tommy Burns, a local Queensferry man who was a very strong swimmer, one night managed to elude the patrol and in the darkness dived off the bridge, plunged into the equally dark waters of the Forth below and succeeded in safely reaching the shore.

In fiction too the Forth Bridge captured the public's imagination to such an extent that when Sir Alfred Hitchcock came to film John Buchan's famous thriller, *The Thirty Nine Steps* he used it as one of the locations although it is not mentioned in the original book. Sir Alfred decided it would make the perfect setting for the hero Richard Hannay's escape from the train on which he was travelling north. And so as the emergency brakes bring the steam locomotive and its long line of carriages to a screeching halt in the middle of the bridge, 1930s screen idol Robert Donat, who played the part of Hannay, is seen clambering down onto the girders high above the river. The scene worked so well with cinema audiences that it was featured again in the second of the three film versions of the novel, which was filmed in 1959. This time Hannay was played by the popular Kenneth More of *Geniveve* fame and the film makers had him go one better than Donat or even Victorian Tommy Burns, by leaping off the bridge and swimming ashore not at the nearest point at the Hawes Pier, but all the way up river at Queensferry's photogenic little harbour!

It is not however just in fiction that the Forth Bridge has had its exciting adventures, because in 1939 the Germans, recognising its strategic importance, made it the target of their first bombing raid on Britain in the Second World War. On the morning of 15th October, German reconnaissance aircraft were spotted high above the Forth. They disappeared before they could be challenged, but shortly after two o'clock that afternoon the air raid sirens wailed again. This time an entire flight of enemy bombers was reported flying in formation from the North Sea up the Forth Estuary towards the bridge. At Turnhouse Aerodrome the City of Edinburgh Squadron of the RAF was scrambled and within minutes took off to intercept the enemy.

First contact was logged at 2.35 pm when two enemy planes were sighted off the Isle of May at the mouth of the river. From then on Spitfires harried the German Dornier DO 17s and Heinkel HE IIIs as they flew on, with their familiar drone, past Dunbar and North Berwick. A series of dogfights developed and two of the bombers were brought down, one on the far side of the Forth off Crail and the other off Port Seton. The crew of the latter baled out and were picked up by the Port Seton fishing boat *Dayspring*. To show his gratitude at being rescued the pilot of the German

The Forth narrows from three miles to almost half a mile, where it is crossed at Queensferry by both the road and rail bridges. Ian Torrance.

plane presented the skipper with his gold ring and it is still a proud possession of a member of the family, John Dickson of Fairhaven, Links Road, Port Seton.

The other ten bombers, however, flew on and reached Queensferry, where many of the inhabitants, despite the air raid warning having sounded, still thought it was only a practice and stood staring skyward. To add to the confusion just as the first of the Germans appeared overhead, the siren at Queensferry Police Station in the High Street, sounded the all-clear. Up at Dalmeny Station the station master and porters rushed along the platform trying to persuade passengers of a train, which had been halted by the original alarm, that the raid was for real and to get off and take cover in the shelters, but the engine driver hearing the all-clear thought this gave him clearance to proceed and pulled out onto the bridge, just as the first bomber to arrive overhead screamed low along the entire length of the train. The train reached the middle of the bridge just as the main flight of German bombers arrived, but fortunately for its passengers, the Germans turned their attention to bombing the royal naval vessels at anchor in the river below. The three ships were the cruisers, HMS *Eden* and HMS *Southampton* and the destroyer HMS *Mohawk*. As the German bombs rained down *Southampton* suffered a direct hit on her bows, making her the first British naval vessel damaged by enemy action in the war. The hit caused amazingly little damage to

Southampton herself, but sank the admiral's barge and a small pinnace, both of which were moored alongside and three crew members were injured by flying shrapnel. Although their ships escaped undamaged twenty five sailors aboard HMS *Mohawk* and three sailors on the deck of HMS *Eden* were also injured bringing the total casualties to thirty one.

As the train safely reached the Fife side, the passengers, who had had a grandstand view of the action, saw one of the bombers brought down in flames by the anti-aircraft guns of the North Queensferry battery and a further German plane was destroyed a few minutes later over the Pentland Hills to the south of Edinburgh. Within days giant grey elephant-like barrage balloons were hurriedly positioned above the bridge and although the Germans made many other efforts to destroy it, thanks to these precautions and the vigilance of the Royal Air Force, the Forth Bridge survived the war intact.

During the immediate postwar years there was a sustained campaign for a new road bridge, but it was not until 1957 that the government agreed it should be built. First work began on the approach roads in 1958 and the 'highway in the sky', as a pop song of the period nicknamed it, opened to traffic on 4th September 1964. At the time it was Europe's longest suspension bridge and the fourth longest bridge of its kind in the world.

In Europe it is now out-distanced by the Humber Bridge and by the suspension bridge across the Tagus at Lisbon. The Forth Road Bridge is still, however, a most impressive sight and perhaps even more beautifully situated than the much sung about Golden Gate in San Francisco. Its three thousand three hundred foot (one thousand metres approximately) slender central span is suspended from two five hundred and twelve feet high main towers on either side of the channel. As with Inchgarvie, in the case of the Forth Railway Bridge, the opportunity was taken to utilise the MacIntosh Rock as a foundation for the northern support tower. On either side of the central span are side spans measuring one thousand three hundred and forty feet. Taken together with the southern and northern approach viaducts, this gives the road bridge a total length of just over one and a half miles. All of the steel used in the construction of the road bridge was pre-treated at Drem airfield in East Lothian to minimise maintenance and it was to be painted once every seven years.

Work proceeding on the southern end of the Forth Road Bridge. John Doherty.

The road deck with its four lane carriageway and its twin cycle tracks and footpaths on either side, is suspended by steel wire rope hangers from the two main cables, which stretch in one length of 7,000 feet from the southern to the northern anchorages and pass over the tops of the two main towers. The workmen, who spun the cables, were appropriately known as 'spidermen'. The cables are made up of twelve thousand galvanised high tensile steel wires each one fifth of an inch in diameter, bundled into strands secured at the anchorages and finally compacted into a circular shape, two feet in diameter.

The two main towers are built of welded steel sections fixed together by high strength alloy steel bolts. It is possible when necessary for workmen to climb right up the main cables to the top of the towers, as was once done on television by John Noakes, a presenter from the well-known BBC children's magazine programme, *Blue Peter*, but usually they reach the aircraft warning lights on the top of the towers much more swiftly by riding up to them in the express lifts. In December 1995 all of the local emergency services worked swiftly and successfully to rescue a worker, who was trapped, after slipping and falling down the southern main tower.

Back down on the road deck motorists are often surprised to find it is not flat but rises steadily from either side towards the middle. At its lowest point it is one hundred fifty feet above the surface of the river at high tide. There are two separate roadways for north and south bound traffic each providing two lanes with a total width of twenty four feet. The cycle tracks are both nine feet wide and the pedestrian footpaths are each six feet in width. Expansion joints allow the steel plates of the bridge's surfaces to lengthen in hot weather without causing damage and wind vents allow gales to blow through and the bridge to sway up to twenty five feet, again without damage. Constant surveillance by close circuit television cameras adds further to the safe operation of the bridge, the pictures being monitored twenty four hours a day in the control headquarters at the South Queensferry end.

The bridge headquarters building also overlooks the toll plaza, where payments are collected from motorists driving both north and south. A code is used to record each type of vehicle passing through and this is displayed in lights on top of each toll booth as the cars, lorries, buses, motor cycles etc pass through. Emergency vehicles have their own code number and unlike all other vehicles do not have to pay. Beneath the toll plaza there is a giant electric blanket to prevent the formation of frost and the danger of vehicles skidding. Over the years there has been much controversy about the hold-ups caused by vehicles having to stop to pay tolls, especially as the amount charged barely covers the cost of their collection and there is also deep-felt opposition especially from local drivers about being penalised in this fashion as they consider the bridge is just like any other road and should be free. Tolls however, seem doomed to stay as there is a proposal to relieve the ever increasing traffic congestion by using private finance to build a second road bridge to the west of the present one, which has already had to have its box girders strengthened to cope with the much greater load than existed when it first opened over quarter of a century ago.

Other interesting proposals are to build a road deck above the railway lines on the original Forth Bridge, as already exists on the Sydney Harbour Bridge, in Australia or to copy another 'down under' idea from New Zealand where the capacity of the Auckland Harbour Bridge has been greatly increased by adding on Japanese designed extensions on either side, which have inevitably become known as the 'Nippon Clip Ons'. In the case of the Forth Road Bridge it has been suggested this could be achieved by doing away with the little used cycle tracks and pavements and by strengthening their fifteen feet widths utilise them as extra vehicle lanes.

While others argue that nothing should be done to increase the bridge capacity and that the answer is to increase the use of public transport, there is one final suggestion that the solution is to introduce a new super-ferry with a capacity for two hundred cars on each crossing, an idea not so different from that which Sir Maurice Denny was considering back in the 1950s.

CHAPTER 18
ROSYTH TO NORTH QUEENSFERRY

A s Scotland's only Royal Naval Dockyard, Rosyth became one of the country's most famous place names, but the total length of its existence was only three quarters of a century. The British navy's links with the Forth, however, date back much further to the 19th century, but originally the ships lay off, out in the river.

In Napoleonic times at the start of the 19th century, Admiral Lord Keith of Tulliallan, tried to persuade his superiors at the Admiralty that the navy should have a Scottish base on his estate at Longannet, where the giant power station is now situated. When, however, their Lordships made up their minds, they decided that the ships should be replenished from Queensferry and it was not until the start of the twentieth century that they finally agreed an actual Royal Navy Dockyard was required in Scotland and the site on the Fife shore in the lee of St Margaret's Hope was chosen. The land was acquired before the First World War, but work did not begin until after hostilities broke out in 1914 and it was not ready for use until after the armistice in 1918.

Throughout the 1920s and 1930s the new town of Rosyth grew up on the slopes of the hills between the dockyard and Dunfermline as more and more houses were built to accommodate the base's five thousand workers, plus the families of the sailors who served on the ships, which had it as their home port. High above them the admiral had his home on thickly wooded St Margaret's Hope, named after the spot where the Queen had first stepped ashore in the Kingdom of Fife, all these centuries earlier and from this suitably commanding position he could look out over all that was happening on the river below.

The outbreak of the Second World War in September 1939 soon turned Rosyth into a hive of activity and in addition to the ships of the Royal Navy was used by vessels of many of the allied powers. When the United States entered the war after Pearl Harbour in 1941, American naval craft joined the international fleet, which visited Rosyth. The Yanks soon proved popular guests at local dances and social functions with their ready stocks of cigarettes, nylon stockings and stories. Equally the visitors from the USA were the butt of much local Scottish humour. Perhaps the most famous, though no doubt totally apocryphal tale was told at the expense of the captain of an American destroyer sailing up the river to Rosyth. As he sailed straight past the dockyard and disappeared up river an urgent radio message brought the reply, 'but my orders are to drop anchor after the fourth bridge and we've only sailed under one so far!'

Another rumour at Rosyth during the war was that the German's thwarted in their many attempts to bomb the Forth Bridge were so desperate for a propaganda coup that they took a slightly out of focus photograph of it and printed it in their newspapers, claiming Inchgarvie was the explosion caused by their attack. The huge importance of the Forth Bridge as a symbol is also recalled in the Scottish National War Memorial at Edinburgh Castle. There it is depicted in two of the stained glass windows at the east and west ends of the building, where it forms the back-drop for both the British battleships of the First World War and also the early aeroplanes of the Royal Flying Corp, forerunners of the RAF.

After peace came in 1945 Rosyth remained busy and over the next forty years was visited by ships of all sizes from the aircraft carrier Ark Royal to the little fishery protection vessels, which gained particular fame during the famous Cod Wars with Iceland. In addition Rosyth was the site of HMS *Caledonia*, the Royal Navy's shore apprenticeship training establishment to which HMS *Rapid* was attached to provide the boys with experience of going to sea. At the same time at the start of the 1970s Rosyth was the homeport for the frigates HMS *Gurkha*, HMS *Keppel* and HMS *Zulu*. His Royal Highness, the Prince of Wales came to command one of the base's mine sweepers.

Much less welcome as far as many Scots were concerned were the Polaris submarines which came to Rosyth as the only Royal Navy Dockyard, which could overhaul and if necessary repair these grim black-hulled nuclear vessels. In time they were followed by the even more menacing Trident submarines and Rosyth developed a split personality welcoming the work which these vessels brought, but at the same time sharing the Campaign for Nuclear Disarmament protesters' fear of the devastating explosion which an accident to one of them could cause for the whole Forth

Valley.

Even at the height of the anti-nuclear protests Rosyth maintained its tradition of annual open days, but Navy Days were by no means a modern public relations man's brainwave. Back in Victorian times the navy welcomed the public not just for two days over one weekend, but for the whole two weeks each time the Channel Fleet visited the Forth. In 1860 the fleet's visit lasted from 5th to 23rd June and throughout the whole fortnight, the shores on either side of the river were crowded with sightseers eager for a glimpse of the mighty 'wooden walls'. A contemporary account records that, 'thousands of visitors were not only welcomed aboard, but were kindly conducted over these noble ships of the line'. That year the highlight of the Channel Fleet's stay in the Forth came on 20th and 21st June, when a regatta was organised between the crews of the various men o' war. Between the races, the ships' bands entertained the visitors and before they were ferried back ashore, dances were held on their decks.

Some of that magic was recaptured during the summer of 1995, when in July the Tall Ships race came to the Forth and Rosyth acted as shore base for the flag ship of Britain's mercantile marine the 69,000 ton Cunard liner *Queen Elizabeth II*, which anchored just below the Forth Bridge in Dalgety Bay. This was the second time in less than three months that Rosyth had for the first time played host to a luxury liner, P & O Princess Line's gleaming white hulled *Royal Princess* having paid an equally successful call in May.

Both visits were however tinged with just a touch of sadness as they were further signs that Rosyth was preparing by seeking alternative business for the day when the Royal Navy would sail out of port for the last and final time. Such a move had been threatened throughout the 1980s and by the 1990s a large part of Rosyth had already been privatised, but it was still a very sad occasion when with the rain splashing down the ships of the Grey Line finally cast off their mooring ropes and sailed away on 7th November 1995. Some of the naval vessels remained in Scotland, being relocated to Coulport on the Clyde's Loch Long, but for Rosyth its days as Scotland's only Royal Naval Dockyard were over.

What the future holds for the Fife port is difficult to predict with rumours that Devonport will not be able to cope with the repair and refit of the nuclear submarines and that they may well return to the privatised Rosyth dockyard, which has also been given a guarantee of a certain amount of overhaul work on surface naval vessels.

One minor bonus of the departure of the Royal Navy from the Rosyth and the subsequent scaling down of security, is that it may once again be possible in future to visit Rosyth's historic castle, which was engulfed by the spread of the base. The castle sits right out on a rock rising straight out of the river and can only be reached by causeway at low tide. Built in the 16th century the three storey tower is still in good condition. The ground floor and first floor rooms of the tower have vaulted ceilings and all three rooms are linked by corner wheel spiral or newal stairs.

According to tradition Rosyth Castle was a romantic hide-away for King Malcolm Canmore and Queen Margaret, but these royal assignations must have taken place in an earlier building because a stone slab above the main entrance to the present one confirms it as having been completed in 1561. Another interesting tradition connected with an earlier castle is that Rosyth was the scene of an affray between the Laird of Tulliallan and the Abbot of Culross during which the monk was fatally slain. The Laird, no doubt appalled at the outcome of his act, then rode with his servants to the Knights of St John's headquarters in Torphichen to seek sanctuary. This they gave him, but only until he and his entourage could be given a fair trial at the High Court in Edinburgh. There the Laird and his servants were all found guilty of the murder of the Abbot, but only the Laird was executed. The servants were all pardoned as having acted as good servants should in obeying the orders of their master.

Other stories connected with Rosyth Castle link it with Oliver Cromwell. One claims his mother was born there, but if this was true it certainly did not lead his forces to spare Rosyth, when they invaded Scotland at the start of the 1650s because it was one of the strongholds which they attacked and defeated. The attack may have caused some damage, because the date 1655 above the mullioned window on the east side looking down river, suggests that some rebuilding may have taken place at this time.

The Barony of Rosyth was acquired by Sir David Stewart in 1435 and the castle remained in his family's possession until the start of the 19th century, when it was purchased by Lord Rosebery of Dalmeny House. He in turn sold it to the Marquess of Linlithgow, whose home, Hopetoun House lies directly opposite on the

Lothian side of the Forth. Like Edinburgh, Stirling and Blackness castles, Rosyth is now under the guardianship of Scottish Heritage, who also safeguard the structure of the neighbouring doo'cote. Castles often had dovecotes as a ready supply of fresh food throughout the winter and others may be seen at Tantallon and Direlton Castles further down the Forth in East Lothian. The Rosyth one is a particularly good one with a fine sloping stone roof on which the pigeons could sun themselves on fine warm days and gabled ends.

From Rosyth the road leads round to North Queensferry, where it is fish instead of birds which are now the big attraction. For the little town below the spans of the two Forth Bridges is now home to Scotland's fastest growing tourist attraction, Deep Sea World. Britain's most modern and impressive aquarium, it is an exact copy of the original one of its design built on the edge of Auckland Harbour in New Zealand during the early 1980s. Deep Sea World's gimmick is that while the fish, including several sharks and impressively large sting rays, swim free in enormous tanks, visitors view them from a submerged underwater clear plastic tunnel, through which they are transported slowly on a moving pavement of the kind found in airport terminals. Most exciting time to visit Deep Sea World is when each day the aquarium's divers go down to hand feed the sharks!

Visitors to Deep Sea World can also get in on the action as the centre also has a large petting pool, where they can handle starfish, sea urchins, crabs and other small fish. It is also particularly interesting that Deep Sea World has in its underwater collection the complete range of fish found in the Forth and out in the North Sea, so as well as being an excitingly different attraction for tourists, it also has an excellently equipped education unit where school pupils can be given lessons specially tailored for their age groups, during term time.

At first North Queensferry's residents were hesitant about having such a large tourist attraction in their little town, but now other local businesses such as The Ferry Bridge Hotel in the High Street are increasingly catering for the ever growing number of visitors.

North Queensferry is also the site of one of the most attractive hotels on the whole of the river, the modern North Queensferry Lodge, whose restaurant offers food and views of equal excellence.

An oil tanker loads its cargo of petrol at Hound Island, immediatley downstream from the Forth Bridge. Ian Torrance.

The hotel has its own visitor information centre and from its grounds a footpath leads down to the northern approach road to the road bridge.

From there it is well worth taking the unusual opportunity of being able to walk either right across the river or at least out to the middle of it to admire the views.

Choose the footpath on the west side and look upstream past Hopetoun House and Blackness Castle on the south shore and Limekilns, Charleston, Crombie Point, Culross and Longannet on the north bank, all the way to Kincardine Bridge.

Or choose the footpath on the east side of the bridge and look out over Queensferry to the railway bridge and the oil tankers loading at Hound Point. Beyond lies the Firth as the Forth broadens on its journey to the Isle of May where it reaches the North Sea. But that is another story to be told in a future book.

INDEX